Milvia Street 2011

* * *

milvia street 2011

is a publication of
Berkeley City College
2050 Center Street
Berkeley, CA 94704
http://berkeley.peralta.edu

ISBN 978-0-9786578-4-0

Milvia Street

2011

Dedication

With sadness in our hearts, our minds, and our speech, we dedicate this year's journal to Doeba Bropleh, whose stories first appeared in Milvia Street 2008 and 2009 and whose earthly presence we deeply miss.

Fall Harvest
Michelle D. Bernardo
Watercolor on Paper, 12"x16"

Contents

* * *

* * *

Acknowledgements

* * *

Poetry Selections
Chiara Alessi
Pamela Brenman
Rachel Granberg
Shanna Hullaby
Tessa Love
Debby Segal
Benjamin Wiklund

Prose Selections
Chiara Alessi
Mary J. Dacorro
Patricia France
Shawn Freeland
Shanna Hullaby

Literary Sequencing
Eric Crow
Patricia France
Shawn Freeland
Debby Segal

Art Sequencing
Rose Livingston

Faculty Project Facilitator
Sharon Coleman

Cover & Interior Design
Rose Livingston

Desktop Production
Rose Livingston

Grant Writing
Sharon Coleman

Grant Assistance
Stephanie Casenza
Mary Ann Merker

We would like to thank the following individuals and public institutions for their generous contributions of time or funds:

Sharon Coleman
Rose Livingston
Louis Cuneo
Marcia Poole
Berkeley Poetry Festival
Civic Arts Commission, City of Berkeley
Acme Bread
Poetry Flash

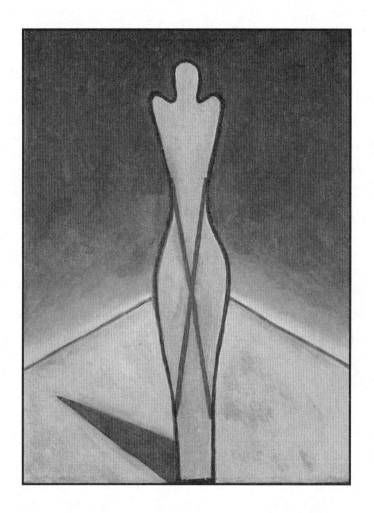

X figure model-1
Jonathan Kwak
Oil on Canvas

Preface

* * *

Due to further dismantling of public education, Milvia Street is currently only able to continue a print edition thanks to community resources outside the college. This issue of Milvia Street was made possible by a grant from the Berkeley Civic Arts Commission, a donation from the Berkeley Poetry Festival and all those who purchased copies of Milvia Street. We would like to express our gratitude to the Berkeley community.

"art-work in mercy's float / is a single song of joy: a man made free"—this year's journal celebrates the re-creation of life through art, through work, whether it's a funky re-configuration of a house deep in the Mission or the rebuilding New Orleans. The following pages are occupied by those responding to disaster or life by blowing a saxophone, weaving a wreath of persimmon blossoms, turning death into flowers and pollen, turning loneliness into writing, teaching their lips anotherlanguage.

The many artists and writers whose work have appeared here over the years have gone on to undergraduate and graduate programs, to art and design careers, to writing and publishing books. A few have returned to Berkeley City College to teach.

With pride for the lives we transform, we continue to publish the work of Berkeley City College students and faculty. Being part of the production and promotion of Milvia Street requires hours of under-recognized work and much responsibility. It also brings satisfaction to see a number of talented artists and writers recognized and encouraged to go further.

We want to thank the Milvia Street Club's officers Shanna Hullaby and Shaun Freeland for their work in producing and promoting the journal. And we'd like to thank all the editors, writers, and artists whose insight, perseverance, and intelligence continue this tradition.

More People Hanging Out
Renate Valencia
Marker on Paper, 11 3/4"x16 3/4"

magick marker
by Eric Crow

art-work in mercy's float
is a single song of joy:
a man made free
        he celebrates
pushes his pen tip
into skin of the sky,
inks his poem like a tattoo
        he chooses his colors
falling mother-of-pearl droplets
across endless royal blue sky:
bold stroke, tigers tail
        he grabs hold and dreams
write enough Nothing
for all to see:
love this wise viscera
he dabs his brush in fresh water
paint drips down deep
to color over earth:
wind blows his mandala away
        he lends his mind
last trace, mark here
as stillness cloaks soil:
plant seed, wait patient
        he lays down with earth
pen dips fresh
in prone figure eight:
square one, right again
        he trusts his careen
push deeper in
find stars over Eden:
there is your place
        he bows

Ephemera
by Wattie Taylor

A puddle so small

remnant of a storm

shines in brilliance

on rain darkened asphalt

Life springs forth

from this stolid paving

reflections of leaves

shimmer and dance

Sparkling movement

enlivens a turgid surface

like a landscape painting

breathes air

to a drab corridor wall

Anonymous Tree
Eric Crow
Photography

Zen Place at Dusk
Eric Crow
Photography

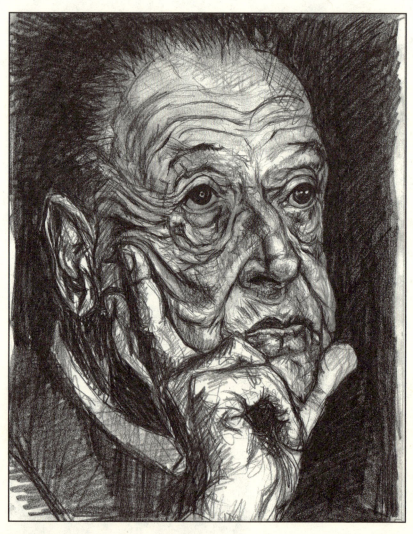

Maughm
Isla Prieto
11"x14" Pencil

The Castle in the Air
by Willy Lizárraga

Vamos, rumbero, que la rumba ya va a empezar
Tito Puente, Para los rumberos

A castle is a castle is a castle y así es El Castillo. A castle is a castle is a castle and without a castle there is no kingdom… was how one of our most popular cha-chas began. We had so many songs about our castle. In fact, you could say that we lived to talk and sing about it. It was the official symbol of who we were, the impossible place where all our stories came together and eventually fell apart.

It had to be a castle in ruins, of course. "Where else can the kings of Latin funk-fusion live, man?" Alberto liked to say, daring us to adopt the foreboding gothic decay around us as our own, trusting that within its crumbling walls, despite our most shameless thirst for fame and glory, we would never betray "our marginal illegal-alien roots."

And you had to admit, it was a perfect match: a funky castle for a funky band. "It was our destiny," as Ali would say as if to mitigate our constant state of alarm because, earthquake or no earthquake, it could cave in on us any minute. It was beyond repair, which meant that we never expected our castle to survive us, let alone become an established architectural landmark in a city full of them, which only adds poignancy to the notion that "it was all a dream anyway," a seventies dream, to be more exact.

So now every time I walk by it, I have to remind myself that El Castillo had nothing to do with this pristinely renovated Victorian mansion, sitting with historical matronly poise atop the highest hill on Guerrero Street. And every time I try to sit down to write about it, I find myself desperate to restore our castle's original down-and-out glamour and hopelessly incapable of it. Maybe that's why at this instant I find hard to resist the urge to quote John Wasserman, the San Francisco Chronicle's youngest and hippest columnist in those days, as if to make my own story believable to myself.

"I am talking," he wrote, probably still hung over from his visit to El Castillo the night before, "about a crazy (as in hot), sexy (as in no holding back) and fierce underground cabaret palace, where you can enjoy and participate, if you wish, in a most non-conventional musical extravaganza, all with a live Havana-Rio soundtrack and set in a year-round Halloween castle on the verge of collapse…"

So, yes, a castle is castle is castle, right? And consequently, everything in our lives before El Castillo feels like a prelude while everything afterward is, at best, a coda, including Café La Michon, which Jesús opened two months after we were evicted from of our castle and three blocks away from it, without expecting that "that hole in the wall de los cojones" would become our headquarters. Meaning that unlike Alberto, always in full possession of an exaggerated theatrical view of life and a hyper-awareness of action as History in the making, Jesús didn't really care so much for symbolism. "Jesús is the silent motherfucker, man. Alberto is the opposite. He's an action hero crossed with a radio announcer." I think it was Cuautemoc who first said that. Now it has become almost a cliché when we try to explain the seamless dynamic between those two: the punkish, slightly Moorish, African guitar and mandolin picking favored by Jesús and Alberto's perky bongo, pandeiro louco, retro-mambo conga style, "the combination perfectation." And one can only imagine Alberto setting foot in El Castillo for the first time and, though all by himself, like a movie or theater director with a megaphone, instantly announcing: "This is it, man, this is the place I've always dreamt about. This is where something really cool is gonna happen." And although he probably didn't go as far as imagining me (or the rest of us) as his posthumous Homer(s) or biographer(s), he knew he had what it took. So he trusted his quick wit and even quicker talent to bring people together. "The rest," as he would say, "is just learning how to keep the groove going."

A castle is a castle is a castle and while we lived in it –lived for it, really —the few things we knew about it came from our landlord, whom we unfairly called "the Nazi" for the simple reason that he was German and we couldn't think of him as a separate entity from Pedro, the castle's monster. The two of them just had to be linked in some dark, unspeakable way.

According to the Nazi, El Castillo had been built in

1896 and survived the Big Earthquake "without a scroutch."
Oh, we loved to make fun of our landlord's accent and we
never believed much of what he told us, yet something about his
heroic, Wagnerian version of El Castillo's saga suited our epic
ambition. So we adopted and repeated it, adding something
new here and there. And like a favorite tune, rich in harmonies,
fanciful transitions and malleable melody, it just kept on
growing, lending itself to unending improvisation.

"Well, when you don't have the looks, man, you learn to
impress them some other way."

That was Alberto's prepackaged answer to our
befuddled questioning about where he found so many stories
about El Castillo, certainly not from the Nazi or Pedro. And
since he told them with such flamboyance, the same flair that
would make him famous as El Castillo's MC Tropical Pit Bull,
and we had more and more guests staying over, often large
groups of them, Alberto took on the role of the castle's official
tour guide.

These were real houseguests too, not party crashers
sleeping over. They were international guests, especially
although not exclusively during the summers. Word had spread
in Paris, London, Glasgow, Madrid, Amsterdam, Buenos Aires,
Cartagena, Rio de Janeiro, Salvador da Bahia, Mexico City and
Santiago. El Castillo was the place to squat in San Francisco.
And we didn't mind that our foreign visitors included a lot of
smart, liberated, sophisticated and adventurous women who in a
most post-feminist fashion insisted on paying in kind our nuevo-
Latino hospitality. We didn't mind either when they became
our collective weakness, and the medium through which we

could exact our most intimate revenge against San Francisco's politically correct, artistically inclined women who never made it easy for us to get laid.

I mean, it wasn't as bad as Jesús' description of Spain under Generalísimo Franco, where sex "wasn't a sin but a miracle de los cojones." But, still, there was, at least according to the media, a sexual revolution going on out there. And we were certainly not getting "our fair share de los cojones," as Jesús also liked to point out.

So, on any given day, preferably the first or second afternoon after the arrival of an attractive foreign contingent, around five in the afternoon, or as Alberto preferred to call it, "a la cinturita del día," he would put on his tour-guide hat while the rest of us --including Nganga, Alessandro, Malandrinho and Macaquinho, El Maca (just in case there was a delicate and persuadable French garçon), plus so many other friends who didn't play with us but just wanted to have a piece of the action —all did our best to play El Castillo's tour-guide assistants.

The tour would always begin in the garden, "the jungle," as it was officially referred to, which surrounded our castle like a medieval green wall. Berries, camellias, wild rose bushes, oleander, ficus, bamboo and birds of paradise were the most identifiable species. The most impressive and invincible of the castle's flora, however, was the ivy. It had completely overtaken the castle's walls and most of the windows, the reason why they didn't open or close. In certain parts, the ivy had even managed to go through the walls and continue its unstoppable growth inside the house. We thought of it, of course, as a most convenient way of having indoor plants without the hassle of having to water them.

There were also two fat palm trees in the front jungle that never failed to provide us (and our guests) with a unique form of entertainment: opossum. Those rather unattractive and seemingly slow-witted cousins of rats had taken over the space between the attic and the roof. And as if catering to our delight in show business, they utilized the palm trees as their own private highway to and from their penthouse. So, at any given time of the day and night, it wasn't uncommon to see a number of them schlepping along the palm leaves like genetically mutated koalas. The spectacle also happened to be an excellent test of our guests' character. If they weren't put off by the opossums' pathetic looks and clumsiness, even better, if they found them cute, Alberto figured they could be taken to see "the Roman catacombs."

After the jungle (and leaving the catacombs for later), the tour would then move indoors, spending a considerable amount of time in the kitchen and dining room area in order to truly do justice to El Castillo's poetic state of advanced and irrevocable ruin.

"Please, amigas y amigos," Alberto would lecture, "pay attention to how these walls have managed to decay with such incredible dignity." And of course, we, the assistants, would point out the different holes and cracks in the walls and roof.

Now, if the decay was certainly awe-inspiring, one mustn't forget that the mere size of the rooms was equally impressive. I mean, you could throw a major party just in the kitchen, despite the fact that in the middle of it you had a gigantic and practically unmovable dining room table that could easily sit twenty people, and set against the only wall that wasn't crumbling, you had three industrial-size refrigerators —only one in working order.

Next to the kitchen, in the formal dining room, there were two ping-pong tables, five useless pinball machines, and thanks to Rosie, a permanent, quite intriguing collection of car engines in different stages of disassembly. They just lay around like conceptual sculptures in the back room of some museum.

Rosie, by the way, was also responsible for the design and construction of what would become El Castillo's most admired and celebrated feature, an astonishingly complex network of aqueducts made from plastic bags and attached to the ceiling that carried the water leaking from the pipes out to the garden. "All very ecological, che," Rosie would say with undisguised pride in her voice, as if enticing us to remember the days when practically the entire ground floor was a minefield of buckets and plastic containers that we had to empty at least twice a day.

"It's like the house is trying to make up for having only one shower, man," was Alberto's take on the leaking-pipes problem.

To make things more dramatic, the pipes that had an irrepressible tendency to back up were precisely the wrong pipes. I'm talking about pipes full of caca. And as if this weren't unpalatable enough, the Nazi would constantly threaten us with eviction unless we fix "the pipe phroglem" because according to him that was the only reason he charged us "so little whent." And he would yell at us in this dictatorial, martial way, subjecting us to an out-of-control saliva shower and implying (at least that's what we thought) that if we didn't obey him, we would be sent to the ovens.

One lucky day, then, a friend of a friend mentioned an Argentinian handyman who could fix anything, from a car to a toaster oven, and was guaranteed to be the cheapest in the Mission. We had our doubts. Argentines, everybody knows, are anything but cheap. We contacted him nonetheless.

To our surprise, he was a she, a tall, powerful she. And when she came in and saw the plumbing job ahead of her, she jokingly said it would take her the rest of her life to fix all the leaks and clogged pipes in our house. In response, Alberto, also jokingly, told her she could move in rent-free so she could have all the time in the world to do the job. At which point she suddenly turned earnest and mentioned that she was looking for a place like ours, "grand but funky, you know, a place where I can have lots of space to store my equipment and tools and play music."

"What do you play?" we asked, genuinely surprised. Her looks and demeanor didn't reveal any musical inclination.

"Yo toco el trombón de vara, che," she said while performing with her hands the typical movements one associates with playing such a long and sexually explicit instrument.

I saw Alberto and Ali's face light up. I imagine mine did too. No other instrument would've elicited such a spontaneous display of almost childish enthusiasm. We had been waiting for a bone like others wait for the Messiah. I mean, first Charlie Palmieri and then his brother Eddie had made it the Latin jazz and salsa instrument. Then Willie Colón and the Fania musicians had practically consecrated it. Understandably, we were so excited that we could care less whether she could fix the clogged and leaking pipes or not. We had a bone! So, Alberto offered her the best room on the second floor even though it wasn't available yet. That was how Rosie came aboard our castle.

Back to our castle's guided tour, and keeping in mind that it was all about impressing las visitantas (Europeans, Alberto had figured out, particularly the Dutch and English, were attracted to the idea of roughing it, while the South Americans tended to be almost too prissy). In any case, usually right after showing off our "tango-mango aqueducts," Alberto would suggest we all pay a visit to "our old-school Roman catacombs," the ultimate test for the squeamish --a moldy, cavernous underground that we thought the Nazi might have used as a torture chamber and that, during the rainy season, lay practically under water. Unsurprisingly, the only ones who found the catacombs cozy were an alarmingly disciplined and pugnacious army of large, dark-gray rats that inhabited the place virtually undisturbed and were highly trained in all sorts of Olympic water sports.

The catacombs, anyway, most often were skipped in order not to upset las visitantas. At which point we would move to the second floor to visit a few rooms, and if Cuautemoc was willing, we would take our guests up to "the penthouse." Once in the attic, we could never resist the urge to bowl, play tennis, soccer or any sport that requires infinite space. It was simply too tempting to have at our disposal all that vast, smooth hardwood floor and almost no furniture to speak of, which might also be the reason why Cuautemoc never really moved out of the attic, even when he "officially" moved in with Ana to raise a family with her.

Finally, as "prato principal," as Ali would say, El Castillo's grand tour always ended in the grand salon, the most elegant, bewitching and solemn of all rooms. Everything in it spoke of a bygone era when luxury wasn't expressed through the possession of electric or electronic devices, synthetic materials or the concept of a functional space. It was all one intricate woodwork symphony: floors, walls, trim, gargoyles, massive beams and a monumental chimney, all in dark ebony. And if for some incomprehensible reason you weren't impressed by its baroque design, thanks to the extra-large bay windows, you had an uninterrupted view of all of downtown San Francisco, the Mission, Potrero Hill, Bernal Heights, the Excelsior, Hunters Point and the entire East Bay.

And since this was "the end of the tour," it was only to be expected that Alberto would use all his seductive ammunition to impress las visitantas, because according to him, to lower a woman's guard you needed not only spectacular scenery but also heart-stopping drama. So, fully committed to his tour-guide role and unwavering in his preaching-to-the-foreign-legions task, he would deliver his last blow to the heart, groin and soul of our guests:

"Queridos amigos y amigas, sorry to say this, but it's time to get real serious. In fact, I'm going to ask you for a minute of silence as you look out these magnificent windows. I'm also going to ask you to travel back in time almost a hundred years and pretend you are standing here, at this spot, looking out, right after the Big Earthquake hit San Francisco. And just imagine how it would be to have this incredible, panoramic view of a city in ruins and in flames. Oh, yes, because, as you've probably read or heard, the fire came right after the shake, and the smoke was so thick that it seemed like there was a solar eclipse. And in that menacing, apocalyptic darkness, you could see the giant flames coming after you. I mean, you might have survived the shake, but now you were going to get roasted. El gran milagro entonces, oh, sí, sí, a sudden change in the direction of the wind saved your ass. And as you stood here, like we are standing now, you could see right over there by 16th Street, barely five blocks away, how the fire had stopped in its tracks as you were about to run for your fucking life."

Lines
Inna Nopuente
Photography

Strings
Michelle D. Bernardo
Watercolor on Paper, 12"x16"

Saxophonist
by Shaun Freeland

held supple straight
slack and intent
only moving muscle
tight slight twitch
of twilight, fingers
and tempo toe taps,
     she stands and
     blows
          out structures of chaos
with a finely tuned caress announces
her distress
          sharp burnt retort twist
          grunt sputter
          squirms her purrs
          desperate
poised and serene she
     blows
          out her suffering
in tumbled scales of wet
tonality,   fumbles graceful
towards   resolution
behind closed eyes she
smiles and presses
her lips and
     blows
her self
empty

Still Proud to Call New Orleans Home
by Jim Barnard

For Carla, Shaw, and all who live in New Orleans,
and for those still waiting to come home.

I

Katrina drowned your city.
BP drowned your gulf in oil.
Interstate 10
sliced through your heart --

through store-front churches,
barbershops and barbecues,
through turquoise houses
generations called home,
through oak trees
three centuries old --

saplings when slaves
first touched your shores,
full-grown when Civil War
severed their chains,
giants when Satchmo
blew his horn
and jazz was born.

II

I-10

Monster of greed and speed
snakes beside Lake Pontchartrain,
an alien, no native of your land.

Columns of concrete his grotesque legs
stomp through neighborhood
now three times cursed
seem the perfect canvas
for graffiti scrawled to document defeat.

III

Instead,

local artists scale mighty columns,
paint oak trees back to life.

The constant roar of traffic,
at least on this October afternoon,
drowned out from underneath
by a battle of brass bands.

The neighborhood turns out,
black and white,
young and old.

Abita, the local brew,

"Save Our Shore" beer
loosens up the crowd
while the profit cleans the gulf.

The homemade praline candy
and pecan pies for sale
that Granny baked this very
morning
in her kitchen down the block.

New yellow, green and purple houses
rise, this time on stilts,
in the Lower Ninth Ward.

The Saints win the Super Bowl.

From beneath the Interstate
brass bands testify -

You're still proud to call New Orleans
home.

Photography *by Anna Graves*

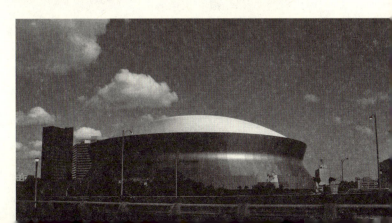

Siesta by the Sea
by Amy Fukuizumi

echo in silence
crash under waves
turn inside out

uncover the lost
left almost broken
call it a wash

feel blue
without pain

salt to taste
as we lay

dirt looks like
earth

and we both
belong

Monterey Flutter
Eric Crow
Photography

Roots
by Patricia France

Unfolded my heart,
it's pierced from the side,
my spirit leaks out.
Spilled on the garden of roses,
the ground groaned.
Pain soaks into the roots of the trees
they kept growing,
filled with my kisses
trees sway in the wind
leaves fall on the ground.
They kept growing, I am surrounded,
spilling out life.
I am rooted like a tree
hands extended up to the sky
reaching for nothing.

Untitled
Michelle Lynne
Drawing

Making Breach
by Pamela Brenman

Slippery slope to hell
backwater lower ninth ward
Tongue swollen
could fill your whole mouth
by the time the rescue boats come
old Perry was dead

Perry had one good leg, but the other was fake. He was raised here in New Orleans—but lost that leg in Vietnam—beginning of the war, '65—stationed in Danang. Perry got the Purple Heart for his troubles and a low rate mortgage in the ninth ward. When he told the leg story at *The Alibi,* it was different each time. In one version, Perry was driving a jeep and Charlie spotted him and threw a grenade under the tire, blew the jeep to pieces, and Perry was underneath it—left for dead.

In another version of the story, Perry and his best friend Rube were on patrol and tripped on a mine. Rube's brains were blown out and Perry dragged himself around the jungle for three days until he was spotted by another patrol and brought to a Red Cross station. That's where he met a seventeen-year-old Vietnamese nurse, Qui, who held his shaking hands in the gray hours before surgery as he drifted between delusion and death. When he woke, Qui said they took his leg and that he could go home now. But Perry always ended the story the same way: *But don't you know the best damn thing is I can be buried in Arlington 'cause of this fake leg* and he grinned and tapped the titanium hull.

Perry brought Qui home to New Orleans after his honorable discharge. But she seemed different in the States—no longer the teenage girl that laughed with the other nurses and patients. Qui got quiet, didn't talk much, and was embarrassed about her broken English and bad teeth. She hated when she was mistaken for the Viet Cong when people found out she was from Vietnam. She missed her sisters, the bamboo and flame trees, and even the rainy season in Vietnam. She imagined that she could hear the neighbor's thoughts whispering through the thin apartment walls: *You don't belong here. Go back where you came from.* She started smoking Camel cigarettes with Perry. At night she'd turn towards him in the dark and ask, *Why these people hate us, man?* Perry shrugged and said, *"People don't like what's different, Qui. When they get to know you, they'll love you just like I do."* A year later Qui had a baby boy. Little Minh made everything better. And she was a good mom. Taught him tieng vet and choi chuyen, cooked his favorite rice dishes, and took him to New Baptist church after she converted to Christianity. After that, Perry and Qui bought a house on Adam Street with the money that his old mama left him when she died. Qui grew bonsai in the tiny backyard—eventually started a little flower business, and took English classes at the adult school downtown.

When the annual hurricanes came, Qui shrugged them off and kept cooking what she called *Hurricane Bun Rieu* while the evacuation horns were blowing, a Camel cigarette hanging out of her mouth. She'd say, *Vietnam monsoons worse, man. One time, my little brother struck by lightening bolt. I saw it go through his chest. What we do? My mother, father, sister and me run like pants on fire and*

27

bring him inside, say some prayers. But he dead, man. That's it, no banana. Nothing like that here. Is stupid— so why I pack up, leave, and come back four hours later? As they say, "Lightening don't strike twice."

Qui was fearless and unperturbed by the thundering shutters during the gale forces of Hurricane George that blew through Louisiana in '98. She just took her sewing to the Superdome and sat it out. This would be her routine through twenty years of fierce tropical storms and Class 4 hurricanes. The force of Katrina took her unawares, but even after the evacuation order, she and Perry thought they'd sit tight. Besides, Perry had trouble walking by then. If they had to leave, they'd ask Minh to drive his car down from Zachary, a small town thirty miles north. Better to just tie down the house and wait it out in the upstairs attic. That night the wind hammered the place. The fierce, growling wind sounded like a wild animal; the rain pounding on the roof was reminiscent of machine gun fire. At three a.m. the kitchen windows blew out, and Qui could hear the neighborhood dogs howling. She and Perry spent hours in the sweltering attic playing gin rummy and blackjack over and over, smoking Camels, and chewing Juicy Fruit gum. The sounds of glass breaking as a tree smashed through a neighbor's window made Perry's hands shake as he dealt the cards. Qui raised her eyebrows at Perry. She shook her head and said, *Jesus, Mary, and Joseph, sound like the big man upstairs pissed off, man.*

The morning after the storm, Qui climbed the ladder and pushed open the attic trap door that led to the roof. She stuck her head out and for a moment thought she was back in Vietnam. Adam Street looked like a rice field back home with water waist-deep everywhere. Qui lowered herself back down to face Perry lying on the old sofa bed. *We got big problem here, man. Maybe wait it out not so good—maybe get boat—get the hell out of here.*

Perry scratched his head, *Whatever you say, Qui-turtle—'cause you know you're the boss.* Perry was trying to keep his spirits up, but his color was ashen. By the time Qui walked down the attic steps and waded in water thigh-high, she knew they'd have to swim to the front door. The dock was another problem—about fifty yards away. She went back up the attic steps two at a time. Panting, Qui said, *Gotta swim man, put on our bathing suits and flippers. Lake Pontchatrain in our living room.* Perry coughed and shook his head, *That's crazy woman. How the army gonna see us if we're not on the roof? We better off staying right up here.*

Using a twisted bed sheet to belay Perry, Qui pulled him up the ladder inch by inch, and they crawled out onto the roof where they saw neighbors hanging out with their cell phones, kids, and blankets. Some dogs and cats too. Qui looked around her neighborhood, underwater and deserted except for the rooftop people. She slapped her forehead. *This messed up, big time man,* she said to Perry. The first helicopters showed up before noon the next day; their cameras aimed steady on the roof people who shouted and waved their cardboard signs and empty water bottles. The choppers circled the Ninth Ward for a few hours. By twilight, they had hummed away into the distance. *Well, they gotta know we're here now,* insisted Perry. Qui shook her head, grumbled, *knowing and doing, two different things, man.*

Three days passed with no food or water, and people's emergency supplies and patience was wearing thin. Now there was fear, disbelief, red anger on the rooftops—babies screaming, kids crying, old people moaning, praying, yelling, and gunshots firing at night. Perry, faded into silence, needed his insulin shot. Qui ranted, *This just like home—Vietnam War. No one come for you. Ninth Ward just like third world country. No one care. Government glad get rid of this stinking place. Where this FEMA?* But Qui knew in another few days Perry could be dead, and she'd be weaker. She had to go now, swim to the dock, get the boat, and find help. At dawn Qui walked down the attic steps. The smell of the cold, stagnant water filled her nostrils and made her dizzy. The murky brown water was full of debris from her house and smelled like raw sewage. Qui took a deep breath and breast stroked to the open front door and out to the submerged dock. Their small canoe was still tied to the post, barely above water. Qui lifted herself inside and found an oar. She cut the boat loose with a Swiss army knife she found in the dry bag. Her legs shaking, she pulled out of Adam Street. Ten minutes rowing and she saw folks she knew bloated in the water, small children, household pets, even a goat. Qui rowed harder towards the downtown.

The first rescuers were way down Raleigh Street. Qui spotted their Red Cross jackets, green masks, and gloves. They helped her into the motorboat and gave her water. A medic checked her vitals. They wanted to know how long she was stranded and were there others? They radioed for helicopters and the news people were on their way. They told Qui to get in the helicopter, but first they would tape her story live. It would be on the news that evening at six. A cameraman hoisted the camera on his shoulder and trained it on Qui's tired, bewildered face. She stared into the camera's mocking green eye. She cocked her head to one side, *I on TV now? Ok, then, this what I think.* She pointed her finger accusingly into the camera, *You better get Army, Navy, Coast Guard, everyone out here. Men, women, children out here dying, man. New Orleans—city of ghosts!* Someone put his arm around Qui as the chopper descended to a nearby dock. Two first responders led her away from the camera. She was still shouting, *Yah, and tell Larry King and Sanjay Gupta to get their asses down here fast!*

Qui led the rescue boats back to Adam Street. She told the reporters about Perry and his leg. But getting the rescue helicopter took another day, and Qui wasn't allowed to go back inside her own house. The next morning the Coast Guard pounded on the roof, yelling—*Mr. Perry Dupree, Perry? Can you hear us?* There was no answer, and when they sawed the trap door open, they found Perry dead on the sofa bed, the stub of a cigarette still wedged between his fingers.

Minh picked Qui up at a Red Cross shelter outside New Orleans. They cremated old Perry—there was a waiting list at Arlington. Minh brought Qui back to live in Zachary with his wife and daughter. For a few months Qui kept house for them and cooked. She played with little Ami. She read the American newspapers. More and more she felt useless and sad. She thought about her girlhood and her sisters. One day she told Minh, *I think I need break from America, now. This President George Dubyew drive us into the ground. No kidding, man.* Qui bought a ticket to Vietnam and bought a small house with Perry's life insurance money. The next spring she walked among the bamboo and flame trees, and sometimes she visited her old sisters still living in Hanoi.

When the summer monsoons came, Qui made a wreath

of persimmon blossoms and placed them around Perry's urn. She whispered, *Hurricane worse than monsoon—You right, man.* She walked out to the bamboo grove and smoked a Camel.

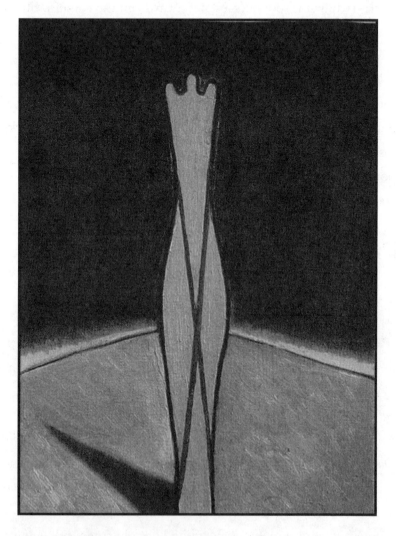

X figure model-2
Jonathan Kwak
Oil on Canvas

Poem – 03
Untitled
by Vinothini Sachithananthan

We decided to leave
packing was difficult
Amma told us to take the valuables
The rest have to be left
clothes, books, diaries, letters
Burn them, said Amma
I cursed the war
We can always get those things back
when it's all over
(Yeah, you wait)
Don't carry his pictures
They would only bestow danger
Burn them
They crackled and curled
Then those two letters
from you afar
You will not forgive me
Perhaps you will.

The moon was a crescent
when you touched my breasts
Then came many moons.
I met others
None was brave
and there was no love
but fire and blood everywhere
fire that was burning through our lives
homes, cities and land
There was no time for love, my dear.

Flies on Poppies
by Teneré Richmond

war
is swatting flies
with hammers,
buzzing frantic
wings on window
pane,
stuck inside the glass
with memories
of nectar
and pollen,
white poppies.

soldiers
carry weapons,
and books of poetry,
standing outside our homes,
they smash the glass
to kill the fly
and spend their days re-glazing.

the fly is free
to roam desolate,
tasting the dead
while dreaming
of flowers and pollen.

Civilian Cost of Iraq War
Matthew Bronner
Acrylic, Spray Paint,
Paint Pen, Oil Pastel on Wood, 16"x20"

Cool Plants Hot Planet
Juana Alicia
Acrylic on Canvas , 18"x 36"

Abecedarius Tropicalis
by Hao C. Tran

Abandoned houses, rusting tin roofs, dead cars litter
Burning trash wafts over coral beaches and blue lagoon
Chewing women spit up red betel juice
Dirt roads crisscross dusty towns
Each and every pothole hurts
Fences keep natives from divers' resorts
Gracious hosts and privileged guests
Hug and exchange *alohas* and *mahalos*
Island phrases overused, abused
Jesuit priests left their obscene marks
Kids say grace before they eat and smoke
Learn in village schools built by the church
Mild manners--docile lifestyle
No longer proud fierce warriors
Old tribal cultures replaced with
Prudish ways of the Christian world
Questions and questions plague my head
"**R**estoring island ecology and biodiversity while
Sacrificing human dignity?"
Truth, insight, or mere flashback
Under the starry tropical sky
Vietnam happens again tonight
Warzone landscape in paradise
X-Ray vision of my past
Youth haunts me like blinking
Zenon lights amid dancing moths

Chuuk, March 14, 2010

dry water
by Natasha Ishmail

i compare your churlish stomp of petulance to my penchant for
papaya pips in namibias land of dry water the fruitless
negotiation of a desert ed past with a more per tinent present
is as tenuous as the untied braids of himba twins patience and
verynice joining in our portion of the etosha pan to scoop the
pips with sepia hands grainy with the silvery white where our
baking reflection is too closely laced to languages stolen before
we learned to speak them exempt from the tender desiccation
still we look to feel ourselves through their struggle dont stir
toward the dust devils in the saltpan today listen to the debate
heated by the tensions of the now namib tennants a wildebeest
gemsbok and an impala convene we tear into another papaya
anticipate that the wildebeest will find the politics of the
gemsbok distasteful instead the impala peppers the plot with
reason it singes sears away at our already dissipating
attachments to a space wind swept by unwilling desertion your
stomps and my penchants they decide cant detangle the surly
bonds of change loosened by new land

Street Lamps
Renate Valencia
Acrylic on Canvas, 18"x24"

Deep Winter
by Inna Nopuente

The every day moves
across vast shadows.
Men, women,
children already hard
at work: chopping
wood, gutting
fish, fetching
water. These gestures
done in darkness,
in silence. The hands
know well to keep
on toiling the earth
to remain warm.

Mind of Winter
Inna Nopuente
Photography

June Bugs
by Rosa Lane

June bugs bomb the porch light--their
spiny legs, date-colored, over-sized. Buzzes
of warplanes circle the yellow bulb in Maine's
humid heat. Fireflies light the field aflame and
peepers pin the night with waves, pitch a universe
that is my mother's kitchen, except I have not
yet occurred to them. She is sixteen, and I will
be hers in less than a year. Supper's on the table
for the boy who will be my father, his eighteen
year-old body, big and husky, but childlike, rinses
away dried splashes of ocean salt in a small,
blue basin enameled, filled with hand-pumped
water from the hand-dug, stone-lined well. The
next morning he'll seine again for Corliss Farrin.
Soon enough the hoarse honk of Pamp's old
black Ford truck will wake the boy who will be
my father, a squawk of early dawn, the first bird,
and Dash the dog, a panting tongue of pre-
breakfast hunger. This is a ride to the Harbor
since the girl and the boy do not yet have a car.
Miley Plummer and Drummy Ferrin,
Corliss's brother, slept the night in the hold
seeing as neither one of them had a woman.
The for'ed gave them a place during the warm
months, the hull rocking small waves of their

sleep, dawn anchored off mooring. Miley awoke first, bolted to the deck, steadied the boy's punt, pulled him aboard, tied the punt to the mooring.

"Beautiful mornin' ain't it June?" asked Miley.

"Yessa, a cocka!" the boy acknowledged. "Guess we're headin' over to Thumb Cap Island first and see if we can seine in a good catch of mackerel over there."

"Yeah, the warm weather's brought 'em in early. Guess their headin' downeast," reported Miley.

"Hey, is Drummy up?" asked the boy peering down into the hold.

Miley flicked the switch and started the engine to heat up water for coffee. This was the last thing the boy remembered before finding himself treading water in a ring of flames and a slick of gas. He dove below the surface with the roiling yellow and orange flames roaring above him, held his breath, swam until he bobbed to the surface at the rim of heat.

Corliss, always late, was just chugging his Plymouth down the hill and arrived just in time to see his crew and his boat on fire.

Men ran to their boats, floated close to the heat, called out their names—Miley,

Drummy, Junior. All three blown yards into the air, found afloat, and hauled bare blistered onto the wharf.

"Get the other boats out of there before the whole goddamn harbor blows," yelled Sprocket.

All three rolled like cigarettes in sheathes of old blankets, loaded into MaCumber's panel truck, taken to Miles Memorial in Damariscotta, 11 miles away. The boy was burned over 60% of his body
--had no way to pay, started to leave the emergency room.

One of the doctors, Dr. Stetson, who would save my life from pneumonia three years from now, came over to the boy and said, "Come with me, June, I have just received a new drug-- penicillin salve. Follow me to my office, I want to try it on you--no charge."

My father followed him—no choice. The salve saved his skin, not a scar my mother said. Conceived weeks later in the heat of that same summer, I appeared in a small spark of night planted in the dark crevice between them.

A Parade of Ells
Eric Crow
Photography

PASAJEROS 2 (above)
Juana Alicia
acrylic painting on canvas, 26" x 48", 2006

Sketch for Inkworks Mural (below)
Juana Alicia
True Colors Mural Design and Creation Class, 2010

Halcyon Summer Nights
by Linda Lu

Glowing pearl above
Shimmering blue silk below
Distant precious nights

Busy turtles left
But the carefree breeze just right
Enjoying the calm

The tune of waves near
Yet the warmth of sand so far
Awaiting the dawn

a cotton dressed poem
by Natasha Ishmail

yes, Oupie i'm writing you a poem
with no words what rhyme
with no fency punctuations
no putting on aires
just
a cotton dressed poem

because you made me big from small
sewed the deep lines from your face into me
your coffeed fingers
showed me how to make my tie for school
the stinging lessons your calloused palms
etched into my action
made me a good man in a storm

the lighthouse in your eye humbles me
my stubbornness subsumes to nothing
but your sober word
nothing brakes me open
like your vermicelli smile
the reconciliation of your history is my buoy
your struggle
my dam against the world

i wonder Oupie
if you will ever see me be
what i want to be for you

but i was
am
and will always be
your daughter

Burroughs
Isla Prieto
Pencil, 11"x14"

The Moon and I--
by Sharmini Wijeyesekera

play
a staring game
nights
that others sleep

Two
solitary
shapes
etched in the sky

out
by Mt Diablo
wind
shudders, retreats

Howling,
the pant of dogs
chase
her down, me down

The moon--
my photocopy
And I--
her hologram.

Polite,
we bow our heads
shuffle
dirt. Shrug. Flicker.

If she blinks maybe I can catch her!

She always seems to win.

Ethereal Mr. Checkers
N. Michael Alfe
Acrylic and Oil Pastel on Paper, 22"x30"

Rubber Bands
by Scott Hoshida

A small, scruffy-haired boy sits on the floor of his bedroom.
Named by his grandfather, the boy inherited the will of the
Hurricane, a famous baseball player who could contort his
body into a spring while stretching his lanky arms into the sky
and flinging the rawhide ball towards home plate with such
strange angles. The contortions, which made batters wince
and tricked them during their first time at the plate, made
most of the baseball league feel that a Japanese pitcher was
a wind-up doll, a gimmick. In fact, the twisting and turning
by Nomo, the deliberate shifting of the hips in such a radical
rotation that seemed impossible for a baseball player but not
for a tango dancer, carved out new territory for each American
batter he faced. He showed flexibility and grace in what
otherwise was a slow curling and unfurling toward home. It
was inside that pause on the mound that batters first began
to doubt their ability to time their swing as precisely as was
needed. Nomo's grandfather hoped the child would not also
suffer from the lack of surety that his late father had suffered,
endured, and ultimately been defeated by, that somehow this
child would understand the import of his naming and thus
become a contortionist, if not on the mound, then in life. His
daughter called him everyday to update him on his grandson's
development, and for this small thing, he was grateful.

Upon first inspection, the boy appeared quite normal,
until a hand gently pushed his scraggly hair to the side and, as it

spidered across his skull, felt two soft spots that might encourage more poking, except that the owner of that hand would know that beneath the soft skin laid the boy's brain and not the pulp of a persimmon or plum or sea cucumber.

His room, which was painted a pallid green, received little sunlight and contained a few toys all locked away, except for in one corner where a baseball caught during a Dodgers game and the mitt used to catch gathered cobwebs.

Nomo, just two-years old, had already been declared by his clairvoyant, tarot card-dealing mother as destined to make his mark on this world. He would change it in ways unimaginable, she said to herself and, when forgetting she was in the presence of others, to the world. He would not just be a prodigy who could draw horse hairs across violin strings or move pawns across a checked board, but one who would divine a source of renewable energy with two sticks of birch, discover a new meditation method to unlock modern-day nirvana, or create a soy-based bacon that tastes like the real thing. She was very sure that the world would not forget her son.

While sitting on a fuzzy, baby-blue carpet, touching his toes with fingers not much bigger than inch worms, he could not know that his mother sharpens his brain by dribbling cod liver into his baby bottle though he protested when she taped bits of cotton to the backs of his ears to heighten his sense of hearing or dragged his fingers back and forth across an electronic keyboard, hoping that one day the sounds coming from the tinny speaker would merge into a crescendo of such harmony, she hoped, to produce water in the eyes of stoic men. Except for the two small holes perforating his skull, holes big enough for large fingers to fit into them like a bowling ball, the boy, because of his mother's ambition and love, had a great chance.

The doctor, the same one who pulled the boy from his mother's womb, who looked at X-rays of the boy's skull with every visit and during each inspection thought about the bowling average he had earned as a teen, continued to worry. When the boy lied down on his side for long periods, his brain rested on one of the gaps inside his porous skull. The soft, twisted ropes of membrane settled into the divot and threatened to seep from his skull in one long strand. Then, when he changed position, the brain re-settled. Trauma, so catastrophically near, was averted. At the very least, no expression of pain ever appeared on the boy's gaunt face, and for this the doctor felt a small bit of relief. The doctor, hoping for miracles though he never once believed in a god, prescribed a helmet and a rotating contraption that the mother was to strap the boy into each evening so that his brain would not settle in one place for too long, would not press on the holes and leach from his skull.

The grandmother, the mother of the mother, would wait by the thin door of her grandson's room, knitting him woolly booties to keep his feet warm, tinkering with a thick, red beanie to protect his head. Next to her sat a skullcap full of silicone chips and electrodes designed to stimulate his mind when his concentration wandered into an unknowable void, and she knitted a protective cover for that, too. As she stitched spirals for the cap, she often paused, wiping his thick glasses clean even though he was still too young for eye tests. The grandmother knitted yard after yard of wool, looping hope into each little bit of clothing, preparing him for the greatness that her daughter believed he was destined to achieve. The gas heater had been turned off to save money for more treatments. A draft of wind glided its fingers along the window's edge, rattling the glass before reaching across the room, touching her knuckles, her elbows, her shoulders, enough to chill her heart. But that organ was too full of blood and of love, too protected by her stubbornness. This son, she thought and regretted, would not suffer the bashfulness of her first son, the one she had birthed and watched and let go into the world without the proper protection of a mother's love. Still, the touch of cold reminded her that she must finish the booties and cap for her grandson; he did not share her fortitude.

The doctor, his white coat tossed carelessly over the back of his black leather chair, crinkled his eyes. He was the one who designed the cap full of chips and electrodes, and who was now tapping the latest X-ray on his thick oak desk with the eraser atop his pencil. Tap, tap, tap. He wondered if he was right to give the mother any expectation that the boy might live. How was he to know that when the boy would survive his first year—a year that the child had only a two percent chance of living—that it would spur the mother to imagine the boy a miracle, a soul chosen to save the world? The doctor pounded the eraser into the X-ray again and again, and as he slowly awoke to his own thoughts, he worried that these contraptions that urged the boy to live—the sleeping sphere, the electrodes, even the woolen booties—had twisted the mother's fervor to save the young boy into unnecessary hope. On his desk a prescription for a sedative waited for his signature, something he hoped would calm the mother's optimism. Perhaps, he thought he should write the prescription for himself. In one moment, her incredible strength overwhelmed him and, then in the next, sent a cool breeze through him. He was a doctor, after all, and she, another patient's mother, a woman who could not face the inevitable. At the back of the drawer, he rummaged through plastic canisters, shaking one and then the next until he found what he was looking for. Even though he usually needed water, this time his mouth was already salivating, his tongue steadily moving the small pill down his esophagus.

The old man who had given the name to the boy, the father to the mother, friend to the doctor, and grandfather to the young boy, owned a large ball of rubber bands all bound together into a sphere as large as his family room. The child's grandmother, the one who knits, thought this obsession strange and meaningless because she did not understand. He stole rubber bands from stalks of broccoli at the market, from newspapers along Acorn Street, and risked shoplifting by grabbing handfuls of rubber bands from bags at an office supply store and stuffing them deep into his pockets. When one becomes old, he thought, there was not much else to live for except for one's grandchildren. When he returned home, his brown pants would be stained at the knees from kneeling in his pursuit for forgotten rubber bands. In his search, he wandered down alleys, opened dumpster lids, and stopped by local bars. The bars were for him, but everything else was for his grandson. His pockets bulged with these small circles, the weight of them pulling his pants down, so they dragged at his heels. At home, with his hands smelling like cheap rubber, the old man slowly linked the rubber bands together into a long chain and wrapped them around his ball. *Yes, yes*, he'd say to the ball. *You're almost ready.*

In his family room, a room empty except for the giant ball of rubber bands, he only had only enough space to sidle along the wall to wind the chains around and around it. A successful day of gathering meant an entire evening walking sideways, circling and circling the room, breathing through his mouth so that the fumes would not make him gag. He worried that extracting the ball would require the renovation of his home. He worried because it will cut into the profits he hoped to make from the sale of this ball. Profits that he had long planned to use to pay for all of the things—the spherical machine, electrodes and chips, soft yarn for the boy's cap—which, according to his daughter, the grandmother, and the doctor, the boy needed to survive. The ball would be his savior.

When the room between the ball and the four walls of the room became so slim that even the grandfather could no longer maneuver around it, he contacted a contractor, a regular at the bar he frequented. An estimate, he told the contractor, was what he needed. The cost of removing the ball, he hoped would be less than what the ball would sell for.

The mother, whom the grandfather called to help determine whether or not demolish the room, told him to roll the ball through the front windows and onto the lawn. There, she said, they could take a photo and auction it through a website. Someone had told her, not the doctor but another reliable source, that the ball might fetch $15,000. She was not sure of that figure, but regardless the bundle would need to leave the small house. She needed to know what balance would be left after the wall was cut down, the ball removed, and then transported to the buyer. She waited at home while her mother sat next to her knitting, the two of them waiting silently side-by-side. The boy slept, his helmet tilted gently to the side.

The contractor arrived in a large, eight-cylinder truck with four-wheel drive that roared like a banshee. Three miniature poodles in the neighbor's yard protested. The old man opened his front door and with thin, long finger pointed the contractor down the hall to the family room where the ball sat silently. Like a physician determining the incision he must make, the contractor waved his finger like a wand, imagining cutting a wall here or there, looking at the room from all angles, from the inside, the outside, wondering if it might be easier to remove the roof and extract the ball with a crane. The only certainty was that he had never performed such a job, that he would never have considered it if the old man hadn't come to that bar so often and nursed a cola so persistently.

While the contractor sized up the ball, this sphere of rubber circles wound one upon another knew that it could not, should not be extracted from the house. It had never wanted to become a savior. The contractor shook his head and breathed through his mouth. The contractor recommended a giant claw, like one used to extract the boy from his mother, metal forceps that punched holes on either side of the boy's soft skull. Those, the contractor said, might be used to pull the ball through the French doors and into the backyard.

No clamps, the grandfather said quietly, thinking the ball might be damaged beyond recognition. The contractor wondered aloud if the ball was worth much, except as an eyesore or an attempt to enter the Guinness Book of World Records. The only problem, the contractor said, was that he has seen a larger ball of bands in a barn in New Mexico, one that was twice this size. *It's for my grandson's medical bills*, the old man said. *I'm sorry*, the contractor said, pulling off his hat and scratching his head, *it's not worth it; I won't do it.* The contractor walked back to the truck leaving the old man alone in the family room. His arms stretched as far as they could go, and he embraced the ball, the side of his face pressing against the thin strands. Had he been younger, the lines might have left an imprint on his cheek, but time had removed all the elasticity from his skin. When he finally tired of embracing the ball and lifted his head from it, the only residue left on his face was the strong scent of rubber.

What is a baseball? he thought suddenly! *Nothing but a ball of rubber and string and leather. Yes,* he thought. *Nomo the Hurricane. Nomo! We will surprise them all!* He skipped around the ball three times, thinking about buying leather and twine, scraping his mind to find a way to invite the real Nomo to help them sell the largest baseball in the world! When he caught his breath, he stood before his phone ready to explain everything to his daughter. His finger trembled as he punched the first number.

When the boy died, his grandmother's arthritic hands had already clenched with worry so many times that they froze into claws. The old man had tried to move the ball to the front lawn, peeling the brittle rubber bands off of each other, the crusted strands cracking and breaking and sticking together until the pile of stringed rubber grew in his front yard as if the ball had spun itself loose and burst through the front window of the house.

I'm sorry, the mother said to her mother and father-in-law.

I'm sorry, the doctor said to the mother before retiring to his vacation home on the Caribbean. Children die was the mantra that he told himself as his plane rose miraculously off the tarmac.

I'm sorry, the contractor had said before driving off with a roar. The next-door neighbor's poodles yapped up a storm once again, that time pleased that they had repelled the noisy giant that had disturbed the quiet of the neighborhood.

As the grandfather raked his lawn clean, he noticed small brown circles that had been burned into his lawn. His world, it seemed, had grown quiet. Or, perhaps, he had lost his hearing? He stood for a moment; his gloved hands rested on top of his rake while he considered which of these thoughts to be more true when the faint ringing of a phone reached him.

Lincecum
Matthew Valencia
Marker and Pencil, 11 3/4"x16 3/4"

And another thing
by Meredith Page

She always has ailments. Some are of lesser concern than others. Of lesser concern: overactive thyroid, sinus pressure, gallstones. Before I'm born, she has a melanoma on her chest. It is removed without complication or need for further treatment.

When the headaches start we aren't phased. Headaches that leave you balled up and retching on the floor are common in our house (migraines). But after the antibiotics for sinus infection and all manner of pain medication won't help, we are concerned.

The first time I'm scared we are at the dinner table. Mid-sentence, she drops her fork and brings her palms to her forehead. The fork clanks to the floor, the dog laps up fallen bits of potatoes. We say *Mom Mom Mom Mom*, it takes her a few seconds to respond.

The first doctor looks at her cat-scan and wants to cut open her head to get the tumor out. In a way, we are relieved. The mystery is solved. The odd location and circumstances of the tumor attracts the rock star equivalent of neurologists and surgeons. This too brings relief; respecting doctors becomes part of our religion. The surgery is scheduled for a Tuesday. She goes in on Monday. We pack a bag, take off jewelry. *This too will pass* she says.

The doctor decides to operate earlier than scheduled. We are still asleep when the phone rings. She wants to hear my voice.

The operation takes six hours. They go in through her sinus cavity, break through the bones behind her eye, and extract the tumor.
When I see her for the first time she looks like she's been in a schoolyard brawl. Her lips are caked with blood, which drains from her sinuses down her throat. She can't speak. She smiles a black smile.

I take time off from work. People are accommodating when you say *brain tumor*. We bring her home and I sit at the edge of her bed. Feed her slow spoonfuls of chicken broth my grandmother makes. We giggle at our new arrangement. How steady I am, with the spoon.

Poetry
by Inna Nopuente

Every day she screams at the world, at no one really, a hollowed "HELLO." I ask her who she is calling. I ask her if she wants to die. She shakes her head like an impoverished tree in its first winter storm. I hold her hand but she does not know who I am. She wants me to be her dead daughters. She wants me to let her come inside. But neither of us know where the door is. Or if there was even a door to begin with. Every night she howls at the world, at every one really, "How long? How long? How long?" The hours linger. The room keeps still.

Autumn Morning
Inna Nopuente
Photography

A Persimmon Tree at Eventide.

by Fred Dodsworth

The bark was smooth, the trunk slim back then when I planted the tree, when my children were still small and my wife and I not long married. Now the coarse surface of my ever-hopeful Hachiya Persimmon is gnarled and rugged, its rough trunk twisted and deformed by my naïve pruning experiments. I call this tree hopeful because I hope to reap its fruit, which is botanically known as *Diospyros*, literally "Fruit of the Gods"—although "Fruit of the Squirrels" would be more like it. Every season a scatter of pale green blossoms grace it, most resolving into small hard green fruit as the season progresses. For some reason much of that fruit plunges to the ground long before the summer sun settles its brilliant orange into the soft juicy flesh of this true berry. Still, come fall, there are usually a good number of not-yet-orange globes hanging and as the persimmon's leaves turn rust red and fall; the tree then reveals its true treasure nearly ready for harvest. But most of these riches will go to the backyard squirrels that arduously cart them away before they ripen. I'm lucky if I harvest a half-dozen fruit out this great bounty.

Sitting in my backyard watching the earth nibble on the sun, listening to the hum of my beehive overhead to the north and the gentle clucking of my chickens to the south, it's hard to accept that these days, my days, are winding down. I've never hated winter. Its cold heart instills no fear. I've never needed spring's optimism and rebirth to warm me up. But now I know the passage of time, and how brief is our moment in the sun, how transient the juicy wet mouthful of the flesh of fresh ripe fruit, and the promise of persimmons yet to come. That said, this fall, it is good to be home. A hospital is no place to spend one's waning days.

Everything changes in a moment. It's a cliché, but true. One moment she felt a small, insignificant discomfort, the next my wife was surrounded by the immediate urgency of triage – an entire team of nurses and doctors singularly focused on keeping her alive. The intense professional commitment of those green-cloaked masters of the mysteries of medicine was both reassuring and frightening. That she might need their undivided attention would have been a terrifying experience if she had been in any condition to be cognizant of their ministrations. But cleverly they had already administered a simulacrum of morphine into her bloodstream to ensure that her growing awareness of this inconceivable pain was stunted. It wasn't that she couldn't feel the pain—it was there like an insistent lover who didn't dare leave her side—but it was obscured in a fog of false memories and misunderstandings. "Where am I?" she asked. "Why can't I just go home?" With her pain, if not abated at least misplaced, it was hard to explain why all this medicinal mystery was necessary. "I think I don't want to participate in this medical trial?" she said. "Have I, through some deviousness, asked for this to be inflicted on me?" her eyes wondered. "Don't allow them to perform these atrocities on my being," she never whispered. "Or am I simply dreaming?" was always at question for my wife of thirty-three years, in the emergency room with a life-threatening condition brought on in a moment without warning. What I called my life was fluttering away like a brown tree-dropped leaf lifted lightly by a late summer wind.

Day slid sloppily into night and back into day again with only the bright lights of a three-ring circus, and lion tamers, and sword swallowers, and giant flaming rings of fire to divide one moment into the next, one circus tent from another. *It's 2 a.m. in the I.C.U.* Time to light up tonight's big show with gurneys and bells and beeps and shouts and screams and tubes running anywhere and everywhere. Incomprehensible growls and guttural grunts fill night's darkest hours, for hours on end. *It's 3 a.m. Wake up! It's time for your pain-pill. Do you feel any pain? It's 4 a.m. Here's a needle*, let us jam it straight into your eye or your heart or maybe your brain. We need to suckle on your fever dreams. *It's 5 a.m. Are you hungry? You can't eat. Would you like some chips of ice? It's 6 a.m. Time for Rounds.* Mystery performers crowd the ring, vying for attention, ignoring the dying. Who could know what transpires beneath the flesh in such circumstance? There, just under the skin, that which is most vital lays hidden, far from view, from knowing.

Was she there one day or one month, or was she even there at all? I could not say and in the end it did not matter. All the ritual ceremonies and sacred concoctions were for naught. As it always is, in the end, it is just one person and the void, staring at each other, waiting for something unimaginable to happen. The professionals surrendered their power, put aside their costumes and potions and magic rattles and waited for whatever came next. In the end, it was time to go home.

Sitting in the eventide underneath my beautiful persimmon tree with its large, hard, shiny leaves of green, I listen to the chickens squabble, each testing the temporary hierarchy in the henhouse while wild birds twitter and flitter from branch to branch, sneaking to steal such chicken scratch as might allow them to raise just one more fledgling to feather this year. It's late and soon the moon will rise, but while there's still some sun left in the sky the last flight of bees hurry from flower to flower in a mad dash to collect a just little more nectar before they too must surrender to what bees call sleep. Their work is fruitful this year. The persimmons hang heavy, hard and green from my tree. With some luck I might taste this harvest, too. I reach out and take her hand. It is good to be home.

Bockchoy *(left)*, **Green Onion** *(right)*
Josephine Tsay
Drawing

Sushi
Matthew Valencia
Acrylic on Canvas, 16"x20"

Letters
by Carla Kandinsky

During the nightwatch
I dip my pen in ink,
let it soak up darkness
so I can write notes
to a lover who doesn't
exist, phantom, always
travels away from me
in silence. He visits cities
filled with music, sends
me no postcards
which I read at dawn
drink a solitary
cup of coffee, wait
for evening when I
can light candles inside
my room, bow down
once again to night.

Waiting
Michelle D. Bernardo
Watercolor on Paper, 16"x12"

Sleep Aids
by Laurin Gurrell

Cyanide is the best way to go. The seizure can be a bit rough, but it's a quick second before you slip off. The other more common poisons you find lying around take too long and make you sick before they get the job done.

There are more physical ways. Slitting your wrist isn't so bad once you get used to it. It's actually quite amazing feeling yourself being drained away till you're all out, but in the morning I'll wake up cold and the mess is a huge chore. I did use a toaster in a bathtub once. It made my fillings pop out and the neighbors in the building were upset that they woke up late because the power outage made it so their alarm clocks didn't go off.

Hanging is no good; I will stay dead until someone finds me. It was very awkward when I couldn't find any other way one night, and I was so tired I was seeing shapes of voices and degrees of colors coming out of white empty walls. Without a thought for the morning, I ended up looping an old leather belt around my closet rail, slipping my neck into it, and sitting down. It was difficult when I cut off my air supply—my body felt the need to keep itself alive, as if it forgot what I needed to do. My hands grabbed at the strap, and I kicked my legs about in order to keep myself from standing up. I felt my larynx collapse as I fought against trying to gasp for air. No air came. My eyes closed. I died. And stayed dead longer than I meant to. My alarm went off at its set time, but I couldn't wake to get it.

Terrance had just moved into the house a couple of

months before. We saw each other in passing; I never had the opportunity to mention my situation. Our other two roommates knew but always skirted around the subject. He got up to ask me to turn off my alarm. He received no answer when he knocked, so he entered and found my bed empty. He turned around after switching off the alarm on the other side of my room and found me hanging in the open closet almost sitting on the floor.

He of course went about trying to save me, not knowing I had been that way for six hours. After lifting my head up out of my makeshift noose, he laid me out on my back, tilted up my chin and breathed into me.

With his open mouth on mine I woke with wide eyes and screamed. He shot back and crashed into my closet wall.

"What time is it?"

"You were trying to kill yourself!"

"I wasn't trying." I looked to my clock, and a red 8:27 mocked me. "I'm going to be late for work."

He followed me out of the closet, out of my room, and if I hadn't closed the door in his face, he would have into the bathroom as well.

I turned on the shower as he yelled through the door, "Why would you try to kill yourself?"

"I told you I didn't try."

"There are people who can help you, you know."

I opened the door just enough to poke my face through, "The only people who can help me are people with cars who can give me a ride to work."

"I have a car."

"Great," I closed the door.

As my hair saturated the back of my shirt, I told him of my added step in my nighttime rituals while I ripped pieces of bagel and forced them down my throat. He didn't accept it. I told him to ask our other roommates if he didn't believe me. I even offered him my father's number.

"When did it first start?" he asked when his skepticism began to subside.

I scratched my head, "I always had trouble sleeping," twisted my lip, "When I was sixteen, I stopped."

"Having trouble?"

"No, sleeping." I paused to chew. "I went over a month without a wink."

"What did that do?"

"I went insane. I talked to inanimate objects. Thought lights were trying to eat me, and everyone who loved me turned into monsters." I stuffed the last of the bagel into my mouth. We passed buildings close to the one I worked in, and I sped up the story, "Soooo… I climbed to the roof of my house to get away from the monsters. Below I saw white clouds that radiated warmth, beckoning me to fall into them." I looked out the windshield seeing the scene play itself out in the morning sky. "So I did. But I ended up hitting the driveway."

"What did your parents do?"

"I don't know. I was dead. Make a left here."

"You never asked them?" he turned the wheel.

"I knew they didn't want to tell. I woke in the morgue—well rested and as sane as any teenage girl could be. I'll get out here."

Before the light could change, I jumped out of the

car. He rolled down the window and asked, "Do you need me to pick you up later?" The light changed.

"No, I'll take the bus."

"It won't be any trouble," he lied as cars honked behind him.

"I'll be fine."

Later that day, I listed in my mind the people who had seen me dead besides doctors and nurses: my mother, my dad, a cousin, my best friend Carmen and one boyfriend who soon after broke up with me. It was similar to the list of people who had seen me naked. Terrance and I only just met, and he had seen it before he knew about it. I had told many people, more that I wish I had—some in preparation in case they found me in that state and some as a macabre conversation starter. He was the first to take me seriously who didn't respond with the fact that the had trouble sleeping sometimes too. For these reasons, I avoided him by slipping through doorways quicker and lingering in my room longer than I wanted till he left a common area of the house.

I was able to score a good amount of cyanide and could wake without assistance. Once in awhile, he would ask me how my day was with an undertone that I couldn't tell was there or if I was imagining it. I would try to laugh him off or say as little as possible, as if I were guarding a secret that I was afraid to blurt out.

Soon I fell into a disposition that I would from time to time stumble into. A desire to live would grow so strong in me that I wouldn't want to kill myself even for the sake of sleep. The first night it began, Terrance came home from the bar sometime around three and asked me why I was still up. I told him my book was really good. It wasn't. I picked something hoping that I might be bored to death. Instead I was two hundred and sixteen pages-deep into *Tess of the D'Urbervilles*.

The second night, he didn't come home. But he was he was sitting on a stool at the counter that looked into the kitchen when I walked in from work.

"How was *your* night?"

"Why do you ask?"

That was a good question. Why did I ask? Because I knew he didn't come home. How did I know? "Just making conversation?"

His elbows slid out and his head sank to the counter. "I slept with a regular last night."

"A what?"

"A regular: someone who is always at the bar."

I had never been to Terrance's work and pictured a woman sitting at the bar hoping the dim lights hid her age as she gave him a sloppy drunk, come hither look. "How old was she?"

"I don't know. Our age I guess."

"Oh."

He continued explaining his situation with slight perplexity. "She is going to be there tonight for her friend's birthday, and I don't want to deal with it."

"Well, why don't you pick up some other girl and leave with her?"

One of his eyebrows went up, "One—you say that as if I'm guaranteed if I try. And I'm also not that type of—"

"Ok then." I interrupted then paused. I wanted to ask if he wasn't that type of guy, then why did he sleep with this girl in the first place. Instead I looked for a solution for him, "I don't have to work tomorrow. I'll get my friend Carmen to come out to your bar with me. If you can't find someone else, you can pretend to pick me up."

"That could work. You don't mind?"

"We were going to drink and talk shit somewhere tonight. Might as well be a place where I might get a comp drink here and there," I so subtlety hinted.

"Right! Of course."

When we got home from the bar, I was two types of dizzy: the drunken one overpowered the one I felt from lack of sleep. I sat at the edge of my bed, arms straight beside my hands grasping the mattress; the bed rotated in the opposite direction that the room was spinning in. I knew how to end this. I looked at the vial and thought of the fun I had that night and how it could all end with a small amount of this powder.

A slight knock broke my trance.

"Yes," I answered.

"Do you want some coffee?" He read my mind before I could form the thought.
I leaped off my bed, not knowing how gravity would have its way with me. Terry caught me for at least the fifth time that night. "Don't laugh at me. You aren't more drunk than me. You should be drunker." He laughed again and led me out of the doorway.

We sipped coffee in the living room as we talked about random topics. Several times he thanked me for going to the bar even though it turned out it wasn't necessary as the girl had a date. I assured him I had fun. I was sure Carmen had a great time as well; she had left with one of his coworkers. As the room stopped rotating, he dozed off on the couch. I turned on the TV. I would have rather read a book, but that would have been impossible on a third sleepless night. The letters and the lines would have moved in different directions, and I would end up reading the same line over and over again till it embedded in my head and I couldn't get it out. Soon TV would be too much to handle; this night I was lucky after an infomercial for CDs of classic country songs complied by Time Life; *Hunt for Red October* came on followed by *M*A*S*H* reruns.

The next night I lay on my bed with the vial of cyanide cradled in a fist at my chest. I had been through worse but knew what was coming if I didn't take my poison. I didn't know why my pillow was wet, and I was too tired to lift my head to find out. Terrance opened my door and asked what was wrong.

"Nothing. Why?"

"I can hear you crying in my room."

"I didn't know you were home."

He rested a hand on my leg after taking a seat at the end of my bed and asked me when the last time I slept was.

"Why so long?"

"I don't want to kill myself anymore."

"But you need to sleep."

My sobs turned into wails as I pressed my sunken eyes into my pillow. His hand moved to my back and rubbed in circles. "Do you want me to help?"

"What could *you* do?"

"I don't know." His hand stopped but stayed on my back. "I guess I could kill you."

I turned over to him, "You would do that for me?"

"I guess. I could. I don't want to—"

"I couldn't ask—"

"You're not. I'm offering."

I tapped my fingers in a row on my stomach; the soft drumming became our countdown.

"How do we do this?"

On my back with a pillow under my head, my hands on my stomach, I warned Terry that I would struggle and maybe should be tied down. Insisting that wouldn't happen, he took my other pillow and knelt over me. "Have you ever done this before?"

"No, have you?"

"What no!" clenching his eyes he shook his head, "Of course not."

We looked away from each other in opposite directions. In chorus we took a deep breath and came back to eye contact.

"Are you sure you'll wake up?"

"Only do it if you're sure."

He took a gulp of air then pressed the pillow over my face. I laid waiting, thinking that I would never run out of air. I got at least halfway through a song in my head, at its bridge— It's abrupt when the air runs out. My body twisted as my legs thrashed about; my toes curled under while my heels tried to dig into the mattress. I grabbed and scratched at his arms feeling bits of his skin gather under my fingernails. His elbows remain rigid as he pushed down harder at the very edges of the pillow trying to keep the middle over my face soft—trying to make me comfortable as he took my life. I smiled and slipped away.

Ears
Renate Valencia
Charcoal and Pencil
11 3/4" x 16 3/4"

Tears
Michelle Lynne
Drawing

sleeping bags
by Heidi Cooper

i remember when she
used to bring home
old dirty men who
she called friends
they lived in our basement
eating mac & cheese while
watching wrestling on TV

if they were good
they might wash
the dishes/mow the lawn
wait for "thank you."
if they were bad
they might steal
her jewelry/kick the dogs
deny it all & runaway.

when my
sleeping bags
disappeared
she told me she
gave them to the
men in the city,
said they needed
them more.

Portrait of Herschel
by Heidi Cooper

he runs miles in the wild woods,
chops lumber with Virginia heat
for winter months long away.
comes back home to drip sweat
onto a clean kitchen floor,
sit down to devour lunch:
five eggs, two moldy bagels,
chunks of old ham & a dill pickle,
all drizzled in butter & honey.

lay the body
down now for
an afternoon nap.

rise for coffee black,
on yellow stained
teeth 81 years rotten.
he feeds stray cats chicken
bones then drives alone to Kentucky
at four in the morning to visit
his sister & kill deer.

Death and Time
by Vida Felsenfeld
(A Pantoum)

Somebody clog up the clock,
Wrestle the big hand back.
Strangle the tick and the tock,
Drown them in purple and black.

Wrestle the big hand back,
Stop it from pounding its fist.
Drown it in purple and black,
Fire of speed 'round my wrist.

Stop it from pounding its fist,
Crushing what little time left.
Fire of speed 'round my wrist,
Soon to be neighbors with death.

Crushing what little time left,
Years behind in my dreams.
Soon to be neighbors with death,
I look out my front door screen.

At the years behind in my dreams,
They turn to me and wave.
Closer to the front door screen,
Ghoul-girls bound for their graves.

They turn to me and wave,
Dressed like punks, poets--a dancer.
Ghoul-girls bound for their graves,
I search mama's room for an answer.

Like the punks, poets and dancers,
Her room has a bed and a clock.
Searching her room for the answer,
Time, lying there with a stick and a rock.

The room has a bed and a clock,
As spare as the time I have left.
In bed with a stick and a rock,
My mother's lover, called Death.

As spare as the time I have left,
He tells me there's room at his inn.
My mother's lover, called Death,
Would he take me and do me like sin?

He tells me there's room at his inn,
I lie down and take off my clothes.
But I'm not that type to do sin,
So I grab for his weapons below.

Lying down cold, my hand in his clothes,
I crack his stick in half.
Nab the other weapon below,
I crush his skull, she laughs.

I take his stick-chunk broke in half,
Hand it to her for keeps.
Bashed-up skull she no longer laughs,
Like a widow begins to weep.

Hand the stick to my Ma for keeps,
Tell her that Time is dead.
Like a widow though, she continues to weep,
As we sit on the embattled bed.

I tell her again that Time is dead,
I strangled its tick and its tock.
Sit with her on the embattled bed,
As she wipes up the blood-clotted clock.

First Storm Sun
Eric Crow
Photography

Terrorist In My Living Room
by Mary J. Daccoro

Couch potato staring at television
Spastic celluloid's Freudian innuendos
That spin the latest must-have gadgets

News-breaking infestation
Journalistic facsimiles
Reviewed, replayed in circles
Robotic pundit slur

Blockbuster offerings
Age-defying celebrities
Body silicone enhancements
Prescriptive catatonics
Squeeze-cerebral gels

Regurgitated hamburgers
Bacon commercials for mongrels
Hi-fructose smorgasbord
Molding couch potato
Vegetating eye

Anorexic fashionistas
Epileptic en vogue
Mongoloid clones from outer space
Sunset boulevard snot
Wannabe famous sacrificial lambs

Soap-operatic formulas
Love scenes of the trite

Television buzz unintelligible
Dog-staring plastic bags
Too alien to comprehend
Same-old package stories
Morph again as something new

Money-making masturbation
Assault on the intelligence, a constancy
Nihilistic crucible

God-damn motherfuckers!
Baboon kisses on the morning bus
Selling me mental floss
What is your substance?
Clouds are raining bullshit!
Terrorist in my living room!

I don't care what transpired
At the Jersey Shore
What's the fuzz in
American Idol's soggy-dread notes
Toasted brain, remote control
Television wins again

The Ideal Occupant
by Kathryn Kellogg

Circe Mason smiled with satisfaction as she scooped
an ox's eyeball into a microwave-safe bowl and hit "Start" on
her gleaming GE appliance. Everything in Circe's kitchen was
sterile, boiled white, much like a surgery or a concept painting
of life in the future. Circe hated with a special vehemence the
common perception of what a witch's kitchen should look like --
cobwebs, dust, untidy bits of crow's feet or newt scales left lying
around the burners, old entrails moldering on the cutting board.
The image of Shakespeare's trio of ladies hopping around a
most likely never-been-washed cauldron, cackling their chain-
smoking guffaws and shaking their filthy hair in the wind, left
Circe feeling vaguely disturbed. Her own shining brown hair
was always drawn back into a professional bun so as not to drift
into love potions or get tangled up in the drying wax dummies.

She did most of her brewing either with short, efficient
zaps in the microwave, preferably, or else in scrubbed stainless-
steel or Teflon-coated pans. Even with a fridge crammed from
freezer to crisper with matching Tupperware containers of fruit

bat ears, or antique mummy wrappings, or salamander eyes, and with sulfurous draughts slowly roiling on the burner, her kitchen smelled only of Lysol.

Circe glanced at her crystal hourglass ($17.99 at Ikea) and realized her new flatmate would be arriving any minute. She did not relish the thought of sharing her space, but in this recession, the market for her more expensive items, especially the youth serums and voodoo dolls, had all but dried up. Her clients were apparently making do with Oil of Olay and old-fashioned repression. Circe couldn't imagine how that was working out, but as she watched her bank statements get sadder, (meticulously organized in rows of filing cabinets) she knew her beautiful apartment would have to be divided and invaded by some importunate outsider. This is where Poppi McArdle came in.

Circe's local chapter of WICKED (Witches Interested in Cleaner Kitchen Education & Development) had forwarded her a list of witches in need of lodging. Unfortunately, young witches of today's generation being flakier than any other, in Circe's oft-muttered opinion, she got a response from only one girl:

Dear Cirse (and don't think Circe didn't note the misspelling)

Hello! I am a 22-year old wytch looking for an awesome roommate! I am from San Francisco originally, but I am moving to Oregon because I believe a small-town environment is most conducive to my further spiritual development! I am a vegan practitioner and an animal lover! I have also recently taken a vow to pursue only positive and healthy wytchcraft that contributes to the goodness of mankind!

More about me: Non-smoker, non-drinker, no wormwood or opium abuse! My real name is Margaret, but I've since embraced "Poppi," with its posititive connotation of Mother Earth and fertility, as more indicative of my true nature! I own three cats. Namaste!

-- Poppi McArdle

With the month quickly passing, Circe's only choice was to mail out the following response:

Poppi:

You may move in October 1st. Rent is $400/month + utilities. Your room shares a wall with mine, so I expect minimal noise.

-- Circe

Circe's doorbell rang, a terse gong. Circe dried her

hands on a spotless dishtowel and opened the door. When she saw what was standing on her spotless mat, she pressed her lips together so hard they almost disappeared.

Poppi stood clutching an animal carrier in each hand. Each contained a puling mass of fur. A third cat sat on Poppi's shoulder, partly hidden under her grizzled mane of uncombed hair. Poppi herself was an unfortunately overweight girl wrapped in a confusing swirl of fabrics: what looked like a pair of pants under three skirts of varying lengths and colors, with a black poncho over a puce cardigan over a pale lavender sweater over a red vinyl bustier on top. Even with all of that fabric, Circe caught an alarming flash of flabby unclothed calf stuffed into a muddy boot. Unshaved. Circe literally couldn't speak as the girl grinned at her and sidled through the door, ignoring the doormat to leave plus-sized footprints all down the hall.

Later, when Poppi had unpacked various furry creatures, and thrown a beaded red shawl over the lamp in their shared bathroom, *sans* permission, she came down to Circe's kitchen.

"Thought I might have a cup of tea," Poppi said. She caught sight of Circe's work on a cutting board. "Oh, are you brewing something?"

"Lust potion," said Circe curtly.

"You mean a love potion?" asked Poppi, her eyes widening.

Circe replied, "No, lust. One of my clients requires them."

"A lust potion just sounds so.... immoral," said the girl.

"I don't waste time fussing about morals," said Circe, her voice rising a touch. "I am a commercial witch: clients make requests and I grant them, for a fee."

"No matter what they request?"

"People's whims and wishes are generally very silly. They will make bad choices with or without my help," snapped Circe. "Anything short of murder, I will do."

Poppi raised her eyes at this. "I believe our powers were given to us to lift up mankind, not to enable harmful behaviors."

Circe didn't reply. Instead she pulled a young bat out of a mason jar she stored underneath the sink.

"Oh, the little angel!" Poppi cried. "So cute!" She made baby faces at the cheeping creature. "Hello little cheeper! Hello!"

Circe took out a Chinese chef's knife and neatly chopped off the bat's head, easy as slicing a stalk of celery. She caught the blood in a handy saucepan, $10 at Ikea.

Poppi screamed and fled the room.

•••

Circe didn't see much of her roommate for a few days
after that. She noticed her refrigerator starting to fill up with
packages of tofu and more bean sprouts than a person could
possibly eat in a month. A flat of wheatgrass appeared on the
windowsill in the parlor. Sometimes she could smell the funk of
burning sage emanating from beneath Poppi's door. All of these
things she ignored.

On Wednesday of that week, Circe had an appointment with
one of her regular clients, a middle-aged businessman trying to
give up smoking with weekly hypnosis sessions, combined with
a mild curse on his taste buds that made cigarettes taste like
horseradish. After he left, Circe went upstairs to her room to put
away her hypno-pendant, and ran into Poppi. She was putting a
sign up on her door. It read:

YOUR NOW ENTERING

YOUR MAGICK PLACE

All of the letters were done in gold sequins.

Circe stood for a second looking at it. "Magick with a
K?" she asked. She resisted the urge to point out the fact that

that word should furthermore have been in its adjective form, along with the more hair-raising grammatical problem in the first word that doesn't even merit elucidation here.

"Yes, I've chosen to reclaim the word outside of its commonly perceived negative connotations. The 'K' indicates the new wytchcraft, which I spell with a 'Y.' The magick used by the new wytches is positive, mindful, and uses no animal products," replied Poppi pointedly.

Circe's response was a muttered harrumph.

"Would you like a pamphlet on a local wytches' nonprofit? It's got like tons of information about it," said Poppi, opening her door again as if to spring inside and grab a thousand such pamphlets.

Circe declined, but the next morning she found one slipped under her door anyway. The cover picture showed an insanely elated blonde woman stirring a cauldron belching green smoke, with a gap-toothed moppet looking on. The caption read, "Sustainable Wytchery: Magick with a Conscience!" Underneath the title was a pink Post-It from Poppi: "Just opening the dialogue!" Circe threw it in the rubbish bin.

•••

Over the next few weeks, Circe found no respite from her irritating new lodger, for the simple reason that Poppi never seemed to leave the flat. Her source of income remained a mystery – Circe never witnessed her doing any serious work, leading her to suspect total parental support. Instead, Poppi indolently lay around the apartment, usually with her fingers traveling between a bowl of Panda Puffs and her mouth. She left crumbs on every surface she touched, long straggly hairs in the tub after soaking for hours, and kettles full of her half-hearted attempts at potions for days at a time. The upstairs hallway reeked of cats and litter boxes, a stench no amount of noxious incense could ever cover. Once in a while Circe would come downstairs to see Poppi browsing through books she'd gotten from the nonprofit and then tinkering with something new on Circe's beautiful white stove. Poppi tested her creations on her cats. There were no visible effects other than occasionally causing little Merlin or Francis or Gandhi to throw up all over Circe's beautiful white carpet.

Circe went on Hoovering rampages and dustbin binges to no avail; eventually her efforts lost their zeal. She started holding all of her client consultations in her room, so as not to expose them to Poppi sprawled on the couch with a bag of rice cakes, watching Michael Moore documentaries and slurping with every mouthful. Circe's concentration began to suffer. She tried to stay away from home for many hours at a stretch to feel sane again, and she missed appointments.

One day Circe was sitting in her bedroom at her bay window, reading *Even More Curses on the Teenage Soul (A Third Helping)* when she smelled smoke. She ran into the hall to find it full of purple fumes and threw Poppi's door open.

Poppi was running around her room in a panic, hands fluttering at her temples as if to swat away a swarm of bees. Fire streamed virulently out of a cauldron sitting atop a nightstand, flames licking the green drapes. Poppi timidly threw the contents of a teacup at the blaze, which had absolutely no impact, and leapt backwards with a squeal.

Circe glared at the scene. Then she raised her hands over her head and clapped a single time, like an angry schoolteacher.

It began to rain in Poppi's bedroom.

The flames went out.

"Clean up this mess," said Circe.

•••

Later, Poppi stood in Circe's doorway.

"So I found my mistake. The recipe I was using said to substitute passion fruit juice for the monkey tails, but I accidentally bought prune juice." She giggled nervously. "Oops!"

"Next time I suggest you stick to the monkey tails," said Circe. "Your little oops almost burnt my apartment down."

"Well, using monkey tails goes against my beliefs about Mother Earth, so that's not going to happen," replied Poppi tartly.

Circe flicked her iPod off. "I think that for all your prattle about Mother Earth, you haven't got the faintest clue of her true nature. Mother Earth is a killer. She knows nothing of right or wrong or morality. She eats all of her creations. She is Medea, but without Jason, without motive." Circe stood up. "And she entrusted us with our powers. You think the Furies died with the ancient Greeks? We *are* the Furies. You need to come to terms with that."

"I think you could use some therapy," shot back Poppi. "Work on some of those Goddess-complexes of yours." She turned on her heel and left the room.

But Poppi should have listened. She shouldn't have turned her back on Circe Mason. Too late now.

•••

That night Circe dreamed. She was back in Grandma Mason's house as a child, and her grandma was using her carved oak wand to make Circe float a few feet off the ground like a soap bubble. Circe was giggling and screaming with delight. The place smelled like gingerbread and the lavender perfume water the old woman always wore. Her grandma smiled; she was going to tell Circe a new secret.

Then Circe was no longer a soap bubble, there was no Grandma Mason, and Circe fell crashing back to the floor. In the old woman's place was Poppi. Poppi had a beak for a mouth, and it was growing bigger and bigger. Poppi's eyes were yellow and hard and then not visible as her open beak blocked the rest of her face from view. She was going to eat Circe. She moved closer and stretched out her hands, reaching for the throat. Circe cringed against the wall; she was paralyzed; she couldn't cast a spell.

•••

The next day, Circe woke up with a new sense of purpose. She arose early, before Poppi was up, and pulled all of the collected hair out of Poppi's hairbrush in their shared bathroom. Then she went out, a wicker basket over her arm.

She first went to the apiary and bought three pounds of beeswax, then to Isabella Machiavelli's Animal Emporium, where she bought a pair of chameleons, a ptarmigan's egg, a half-pound of butterfly chrysalides and the pelt of an arctic fox. Isabella thought it very strange that Circe didn't once try to haggle down the steep price – her regular customer seemed distracted and intent on something elsewhere. Circe handed over her Mastercard and then left for home.

Once back in her kitchen, she worked quickly. She melted the wax and formed it over a steel mold to make a hollow wax doll. Circe let it dry on a rack and then cut it in half lengthwise, so that the doll's face was on one side and the back of its head on the other. She burnt the fox fur with a miniature crème brulée blowtorch, and killed and skinned both chameleons. Then she emulsified the skins and ashes in the ptarmigan egg. Circe lined the bottom half of the doll with butterfly chrysalides, squeezing them to powder and pressing them into the wax, then piped in the emulsified mixture with a pastry bag. To the top of this Circe added nine hairs off of her own head, and then sealed the doll back together.

Circe took a look at the assembled figure. She pushed Poppi's stray clouds of hair into the head, and wrapped fabric around its body to form a skirt and poncho. She carved small eyes and an open mouth on its face. Finally she carved the word, "Metamorphosis" across its chest where the heart would be, like a sash across a beauty queen.

As Circe gazed at her completed work, a crooked smile appeared on her face. Outside the sky darkened to the color of a fresh bruise, and a cold north wind began to blow.

That afternoon it was too easy to wait until Poppi climbed into the bathtub and slip into her room. It was too easy to sew the wax figure into the underside of her mattress. Merlin, Francis and Gandhi sniffed the spot, and then ran yowling for the door.

The next morning Circe sat at the breakfast table, humming and eating her toast and flipping through the entertainment section of the paper. She heard Poppi's door swing open, and turned with some interest to watch her roommate descend the stairs.

Poppi moved slowly, looking straight ahead of her. Her hair was done up in a professional bun, her clothes single-layer. She walked to the refrigerator and pulled out a rasher of bacon, slit the packaging and threw four strips onto a George Forman grill. "Can I get you any bacon?" she asked Circe, but slowly, as one might speak in a dream. Circe looked for a second into Poppi's strangely fixed eyes and nodded in recognition. "Good morning." Two Circes greeted one another.

Cerrito Theater
Matthew Valencia
Marker and Pencil, 11 3/4"x16 3/4"

Berry & Berkeley
Matthew Valencia
Acrylic on Canvas, 20"x24"

Sonnet at Polk & Ellis
by Mary K. Senchyna

He was found in bed with a rope around his neck
naked from the waist down, sperm lacing his fingers
bed sheets swollen with the last scent of him.
We were both twenty-four that year but had never met.
He lived in the basement apartment, I in the studio on the top
floor.
Between us the manager, an ex-priest who at night adorned
in musty Franciscan robes anointed the boys on Polk Street.
The entrance to our 1920s building, a straight railroad car hall,
was shrouded
like a gothic thrift store; crimson walls, gilt-framed Jesuses,
knowing-eyed
shepherds, wisps of frankincense circling like an Easter mass.
His father came from the center of the country, maybe Kansas
It was mid-month and he couldn't afford a hotel.
At night his steady sobs rose up through the shaft
as he packed his son's life into boxes to carry him home.

jew among jews
by Rachel Marcus

everywhere, in cities,
jews in long skirts, in hats, walk home from synagogue
after services
on rosh hashanah morning.
the shofar squeaks and uproars
hiccups sarcastic
like jews
through all humanity.

my father watches the game on saturday,
claws at the circular raisin challah,
all for him.

i have found some nice clothing—
tights that pull at my leg hairs,
borrowed shoes a size too small,
lock my bike, make my way up

and the voices
sound harmony into the ether
burst the sturdy ceiling off this temple
oh brand new day! god, we are here,
we are magical!
the voices
pour down to the pigeons, to the high-rises
around lake merritt.
walking the stairs,
my layers peel off,
body as supple and warm as tender chicken

what part of the diaspora, here with me now?
an exodus from new york to berkeley, 1969.
they dance in beads, they dress in shawls, they move in white

offer freely
hips and hands to hashem,
body to buddha

in the balcony,
my forearm connects
bony knee to chin,
i flip through the songbook
of hebrew and commentary.
seats vibrate a tune
i should have carried from ancestors.
it slipped off the bone.
i look for the page

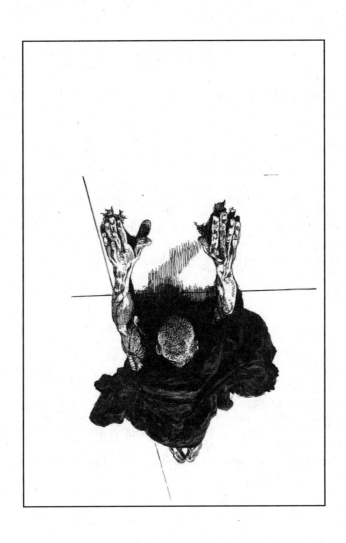

Synchronicity
Isla Prieto
Watercolor and Pen, 9"x12"

Letter to a White Girl in Oakland
by Jess Marks-Gale

Your life has been much like riding backwards on the bus.
Today, you're backtracking through the neighborhood you ran
away from,
a neighborhood overflowing with people who don't look like
you.
The people who do look like you are only here to restore history
by erasing the present, like cutting down a sapling
to erect an insolent brass statue of a fallen oak.
You are not like them either.

Maybe it was not the people that were the problem for you.
You laughed and shouted down the block
in daylight; you loaned and borrowed and loaned
dollars and cigarettes and dollops of butter.
You felt like green fighting sidewalk,
like a weed creeping through cracks,
trying to find sun and throwing your roots down defiantly,
deep into the breadcrumb dirt under your feet.

The real problem was fear.
Fear ate holes through your chest
as you listened to bullets chasing children down the block,
determined as bloodhounds bounding through underbrush.
Fear wrapped its veins around your throat,
stopping your words at the crosswalk
when you heard a man dismantling his wife next door.
Instead of shouting, you shut your window against the chemical
wind
and hoped to dream of lichen and dandelions—
if you could sleep at all.

You felt like green fighting sidewalk,
and if you know anything about the psychology of weeds,
you know that they fight too tenaciously,
vying for any place as if death were hollering
in the dark pursuing them through the hot night.
If you know anything about the psychology of weeds,
you know that all they do is take over.

Leaves
by Teneré Richmond

I learned the art of blending
from the forest
it's a sneaky sort of art
I like that
First it takes seeing
oak leaves mix with bay
a way of seeing
scattered bones
little solar collectors
done with duty
scattering the floor
a ring of stones
fire pit
But camouflage is a funny word
But camouflage
sends me sneaky
strewn

It's really the art of noticing
while you're hiding
or blending, as I said
so an accent can be a forest
when I blend my speech to Spanish
con accento
I am camouflaged in sound

Learning Cuban
by Mary K. Senchyna

I tried to tell you
about the humming birds
that visit the fuschia
I hung on my back porch,
their small bodies
shivering
with the vigilance of pollination
and this simple word
I did not know.

Zunzun en La Habana
Chuparosa
rose sucker in Arizona
colibri en Guatemala
mosca pajaro en Espana

I know the exchanges of longing
anhelo
I have learned its verse
t*e extrano, te falto, te quiero*
I know the soundlessness
of losing you
again and again
how we enter a vacuum the last day
and the mysterious lack of smell
at La Habana International Airport.

I know the long row of blue doors
without windows
I enter each time I leave you
and how our world
absent from the order
the tongue gives
floats across the sea.

CORAZON DE MELON
Juana Alicia
Acrylic Painting on Canvas, 24"x 36", 2009

111

Quest
by Carla Kandinsky

I search for you in old
documentaries, looking
for a man in bell-bottoms,
long hair reaching
his waist, swirling as he dances.
I seek for you among films
of flower children, not yet
knowing their quest
for a world whirling
with wonder and joy
will never exist.
I catch glimpses of you
in the eyes of a man
on Telegraph Avenue, still
selling shirts, bright tie-dye
dipped in colors of dreams.

I see you struggling
with today, a news shot
of you on the shoreline,
your hands hold a net
of sludge and slime left from
from the oil spill. You call to say
your car is filled with boxes of birds,
black-coated wings useless
as you drive them to sanctuary.
No longer dancing, you are
still searching, tending hands
seeking to right what is wrong.

The Rockefeller Effect
by Michael Noel

A click of chips. Thick smoke hangs in the air. Sunday afternoon with the family. I have to be a little vague about numbers because the "Tribe," as they are called by the in-laws, includes at least a hundred-fifty people.

My grandfather deals the cards out to six of us at the table. He deals himself an extra card. Am I the only one who notices this? He is cheating. He is cheating his own sons. Not only that, he is cheating the next generation, which includes me. I think a moment and try to reckon how much must be in the pot. It must be forty dollars. And I think I should mention that my grandfather has made a "mistake," as I would label it. And I would say this except, except for one thing, my grandfather either by accident or design has dealt me a full house. My heart is going. My voice pops up an octave. I try to breathe in a slow regular manner.

I think about my options. People are talking. Two conversations are going on at the table, the usual one, about how stupid and corrupt the government is, and a second theme is woven in, something about an event that happened years ago.

I like to think I can multitask as well as the next poker player, but the truth is I have lost the thread of both conversations; I have a full house. Finally after all these years, I suck in the feeling of triumph. I am going to clean up here.

Uncle Ray looks at me. He has a booming voice that shakes the table, "What do you got there, kid? Got two pair?"

"You are going to have to pay to find out," I have been waiting for this moment for about fifteen years.

He sucks a worn drag on the last of his cigarette and stamps it out in the tired old ashtray. His face is a crumpled map of wrinkles. His forehead alone could provide the lines for an atlas of blue highways—little side roads are mapped there. There are crow's feet at the corner of his eyes that have their own wrinkles.

I look at my cards and try to keep breathing in a slow regular pace. I am not going to tip this hand.

A stray thought pops into my head for a moment: why I am in this family when there are already enough people for a baseball game and a small crowd of fans in the stands? This has recently been manifest at the picnic.

I wonder to myself if the Rockefellers spend their afternoons like this. I wonder how I would have been different if I had born into the Rockefeller family? It's worth considering.

"Has anyone ever read about how bad smoking is for you?" I ask the room. I wave my hand in front of my face. "You know, none of the Rockefellers smoke." My entire family are lifelong Democrats. Am I the only one who has contemplated the wisdom of businesslike Republicans?

"You think you're smarter than your old uncles, don't you? Ray finally says.

"Well, not to brag, but I am a college graduate," I think it's reasonable that I point this out every once in a while. Ray looks at me and at the cards in my hand as if he possesses x-ray vision.

"Great, well I think you got two pair." He throws in a

chip. "You got the education but we have the experience," he says for the fiftieth time, or is it the five hundredth?

My grandfather, seventy-six years old, built this house we are in. His offspring flood this place; he is from a war-torn European country; he has been a translator for the United States Army; he can quote Shakespeare; he can name the capitols of all the states. He looks like someone has carved him out of a stack of bricks. I feel like a flabby young slacker next to him. He can do more in a day than I can do in a week. And in his spare time, running a dairy farm, he has found time to father, clothe and feed fifteen children. His green eyes look at the pile of wrinkled dollars, at the poker face I have carefully prepared. Talk about experience, wisdom comes forth as he speaks.

"The Rockefellers can kiss my ass," he says louder than needed. "I suppose it would be too much to ask, for you to take your damn turn, play your damn card, and stop worrying about the God damn Rockefellers."

Everyone laughs. He laughs a joyous bellow. It's the laugh of Zeus. No one recalls my grandfather composing a sentence without using the word "damn" in it. Grammatically it is remarkable. He can use "damn" as a verb, an adjective, and an adverb. He has even been able to use it to modify itself. It's impressive exercise in English expression that I admire.

My uncle Ray turns to his brother, "You owe the pot more dollars," and Glenn throws several more dollars in the pot.

"You bet a dollar on every time he said 'damn'? It's incredible," I say.

I'm beginning to see how crazy they really are, but I'm

discreet, say nothing. I look only at my cards. I try not to laugh, and the more I try to restrain myself, the harder it is, in true wonder, not to laugh.

The coffee comes. The beer bottles are taken away. Who is ever up cleans up. It's a rule. And people use it as an opportunity to check into the kitchen, talk to wives and Mother. There is laughter from the kitchen; someone is telling joke in there. It does not distract me. I pull my cards close to my chest.

"Well, what happens to you after Germany?" Ray asks me, already another cigarette between his yellow fingers.

"Then, unless the war escalates, I finish up my enlistment there."

"I bet that damn Nixon will escalate," my grandfather injects. He hates Nixon in a visceral manner that seems all out of proportion. I am afraid to ask for details. I'm just glad to be going to Germany.

My grandfather hates Nixon, and by this revelation I realize, perhaps for the first time, who he is. He grows his own food. He recycles. He brews passable beer. He fits into Berkeley, California better than I ever will.

Now this is where my grandfather shows his confusion because as everyone knows, next year, the eighteen year olds will get to vote. Nixon is on his way out, and the war over. I'll work on a sun tan in Ibiza. I'll tour the capitols of Europe on the GI Bill. Sometimes my family is so ignorant. To tell you the truth, I can hardly stand to discuss anything with them.

Ray puffs away on his cigarette for a moment. "It's bullshit, the whole thing. Stay in the rear with the gear," he says between inhales. "That's the important thing: in the rear with

116

the gear. That's what we say."

My plans don't include Viet Nam. I'll touring Europe, go to Ibiza, hang out in Paris. I ask Uncle Glenn, once an Air Force captain, what Paris is like. This is the wonderful thing about having a large family. There is always someone who has been there or done it, whatever it is.

"I hated being ordered around in the military," Uncle Glenn confesses. " I just liked wearing the uniform, flying the planes."

There is only one person that truly intimidates my grandfather, that truly has the upper hand in his vision of the world. Fortunately that person is busy in the kitchen right now, great warm smells of bread float around us. She is rolling out another cake, a loaf of bread. It's an astounding production that, I must confess, I have taken for granted for all these years, and while she does this, she is carrying on, at a rapid clip, a conversation with great detail and insight with two of her adult daughters. They exchange information more rapidly, more completely, than any of my uncles could communicate after pots of strong coffee. Small wonder she has been able to be the mother of fifteen children. It's unbelievable. I see it, and still I do not believe it. It is not possible. Someday, during the card game, she will reveal in a loud voice, the great truth: all the boys have been adopted from a failed primary school after a terrible explosion. It is not possible that this little woman, who just comes to my shoulder, produced all these large men.

Now she appears in the doorway. She announces she needs milk and butter. Someone must go to the store. Everyone sits up straight. Everyone looks at me. Glenn takes a handful of wrinkled dollars out of the pot and hands them to me.

"Wait here," Ray reaches in his pocket and hands me a set of keys. "Just go across the street. We got milk and butter in the refrigerator." Ray looks at me for a moment, a meaningful glance. "Check out what I've done to the Indian."

"Do you still have the Beast?" I ask in wonder. It must be all chrome by now, I think. It's a classic motorcycle from the 40s Ray has been working on for years, collecting original parts. We took rides on it when we were kids. I head to the door eager to see it.

"Hurry back, or we have to play your hand," Glenn adds.

I go into the kitchen. More of my seven aunts have flooded in filling up the modest space. Grandma tells me what she needs. One of my aunts asks me about my first wife, *again. I can't even tell who is saying what.*

They loved her. She was so cute and perky. I hate perky. That's why we are not together. Now, this is the difficulty with having a large family. My aunts will rush up to me, even as I go to the movies, asking me personal questions or providing unsolicited advice. They can make an awkward situation even more awkward.

"You know your cousin Natalie was asking about you," one of my aunts informs me. "You would have a ready-made family," another of my aunts thoughtfully continues. "Look, he is blushing."

Am I so lost and low, so socially incompetent, that my sweet cousin is my only option? But then I think, who am I to dismiss Natalie? Who am I to dismiss anyone, when you consider it? She is long, lean and lanky with big brown eyes. She has all the things that appeal to the superficial male. She has a job and a pickup truck. She is smart, funny, and her husband has mysteriously vanished. Strangest of all, she likes me. We have a lifetime of people to talk about.

It's a few steps to Ray's home. My cousin Natalie greets me at the front door. She is swinging one of her small children on her hip. She smiles her great neon smile.

"He said he wanted you to see the bike?" She asks as if this surprises her. She looks at me in a meaningful way. I wonder at the way she balances her youngest child while her oldest peeks out at me from behind her legs. They are beautiful children, small quiet blonds with big brown eyes. She gestures towards the door and walks over to it. I open the door, feel for the light switch and wait for the reflection from the Indian to catch my eye.

It's gone! The Bike! Completely gone!

In its place is a horticultural explosion of green. There are forty or fifty marijuana plants as tall as my head. There is a hum of hydroponics. The walls are covered with insulated foil. Small grow lights are shinning small narrow beams like a revelatory science fiction movie.

I observe with shallow breathing. I look as I imagine Balboa most have stared, stunned "high on a peak in Darien," at his first glimpse of the Pacific, a new ocean rolling on forever. The place reeks. What in the hell is this? My mind and stomach pop out of my body for a moment.

Natalie looks at me. Then, in a sudden move that a Judo master would admire or a teacher would perform on school children, she slings her infant to her left hip, pulls me towards her with her right arm. Squeezing the milk and the cubes of butter between us, she gives me a kiss that I can only describe as meaningful.

"Just remember why you are over there," she smiles, the neon brightness returns to her face. I think we agree to get together tomorrow, but who the hell knows. I waddle back across the street in a kind of daze. I leave the country for a few months and the entire blue sphere has popped into a new orbit.

Smell tentacles of bread aroma reach out to the card table in the front room. I slip out of the kitchen without being ensnared by aunts.

I return to the card table. There is a pile of wrinkled dollars, fifty-six bucks at my place. My grandfather is shuffling the cards, ready to deal again. I pocket the money with the pure joy of being alive. My grandfather looks at me for a moment. "You probably want to wipe that damn lipstick off," my grandfather says. He looks at Ray, but Ray is not concerned about who kissed who.

Ray looks over at me, "How did you like what I've done to the bike?"

"Looks better than I imagined," I keep a poker face and I hope a normal cadence in my voice, but my pulse is racing in wonder.

"I thought you'd enjoy it. It's Rockefeller quality," he says, "Just for you."

I think about the Rockefellers. They are worth considering. I wonder what weed they smoke. It's an open question if their life is significantly better than my life. I don't recall meeting any of the Rockefellers at the air force base.

My grandfather deals the cards again. His thick fingers are surprisingly agile. I watch to see if he is dealing himself a second. He deals me a pair of bullets. Everyone looks at me. I put in five chips, take two cards. And the card game goes on forever.

Berry in Kitchen
Renate Valencia
Marker on Paper, 11 3/4"x 16 3/4"

A Poem
by Sharmini Wijeyesekera

Around you words always seemed excessive
so I started stuffing them into napkins
at dinner, feeding chunks to the cat
while your back was turned. Face to face

I bit my lip—little drops of endearment
trickled down my chin but you hardly noticed, too busy dancing
on sentimental singer's
stories. You slid your head to the rhythm as we

both soaked in harmonies of adventure-
romance and one-line emotional satori,
so I swallowed my paragraphs and spit out
weak metaphors to match the mood. And as my

room grew thick with the smell of rotted ideas
and trampled communications (hidden under
the bed, hastily shoved into drawers) I reveled
in the notion that my world was full of poems.

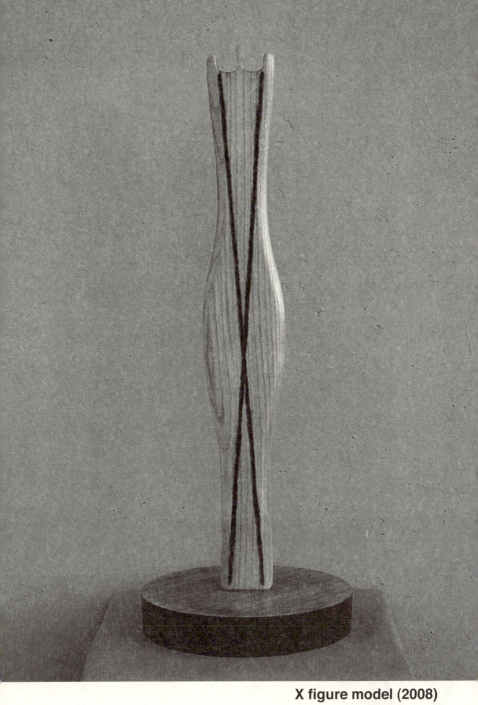

X figure model (2008)

Jonathan Kwak

Mixed Media, 28" tall

un/winding
by Rachel Marcus

transacting in words all day
i come home: empty basket,
none for you.

the tea is shrill in its demand to stop the fire beneath it.
we meander from opposite sides of the apartment

crumpled receipts, nickels, pennies from my pockets
are all i have to offer

across the table
we look to the left of each other.

Cross Talk Noise
by Tsutomu Inoue

You and I were talking over the sea.
You were in the night, and I in the morning.
You talked about your day, and I about my dream.

You fell asleep
While I was talking.
Outside the window was filled with sunlight.
Inside the receiver was filled with darkness.
Except for a cross talk noise
There was no sound.
I felt it was a foreign language,
Chinese, maybe.

The noise escaped from the receiver
And wind chased it
A man yelled in Chinese
And wind caught it
You talked in your sleep
And wind carried it.

I wondered if you saw a Chinese dream.

You and I were talking over the sea.
You were in your night, and I was in my day.
You fell into your dream, and I hung up the phone.

Biographies

* * *

N. Michael Alfe is an independent fine artist has had several solo exhibitions nationally and internationally. He has also worked at the Los Angeles County Museum of Art and the Hammer Museum. He has designed exhibits in museums in San Francisco. Currently he teaches Multimedia at Berkeley City College.

Juana Alicia Araiza is a muralist, print maker, educator, activist and painter who loves to draw. She has been teaching for thirty years, currently at Berkeley City College. Her sculptural and painted public works can be seen in Nicaragua, Mexico, Pennsylvania and California, most notably in San Francisco and Berkeley.

Jim Barnard tries to shine a creative light on injustice and suffering. Yet ending there would miss the courage and inspiration that enables folks to unite and triumph over oppression. His poetry illumines both pain and hope.

* * *

A traveler, artist and photographer, **Mic D. Bernardo**'s passions include photography, watercolor, and acrylic painting, ancient civilizations of Mesoamerica, Greece, and Southeast Asia. Some of her accomplishments include winning a photo contest and being published in the Seattle Visitor's Guide.

Pamela Brenman is a native New Yorker who came to San Francisco State University to study writing with Frances Mayes and Stan Rice. Her passion is writing historically imagined fiction and poetry that draws upon the voices of a menagerie of characters inspired by history, myth, and fairytales.

Matthew Bronner: "This is the first piece (Civilian Cost of Iraq War) in a series of anti-war paintings, covering modern and past conflicts involving the United States. It is a departure from my previous artwork that explored pure abstraction inspired by nature. My hope is that viewers of my new work will be reminded of the costs of war and will be inspired to speak out against such atrocities."

Heidi Elyce Cooper is a young Virginian living in Oakland. She transferred from Berkeley City College and is studying creative writing at Mills College.

Eric Franklin Crow has been writing since he was ten years old and thanks his mother and father for grounding him long enough to write his first play.

Why *Mary J. Dacorro* loves poetry is best expressed by this quote from her favorite American poet, Edgar Allan Poe: "Poetry's brilliant flowers are the dearest of all unfulfilled dreams, and its raging volcanoes are the passions of the most turbulent and unhallowed of hearts."

After nearly 35 years in the wilderness, *Fred Dodsworth* returned to college. Fatherto three children and two granddaughters, and husband to a loving wife, he enjoys his educational experience this time round. The stars not crossed, he'll attend SFSU's Creative Writing program in September.

Vida Felsenfeld is a secretary by day, poet by night, flamenco dancer always. She enjoys reading and writing poetry, and uses it sometimes as a compass to navigate her through life. And in the words of Bob Dylan, she is always "busy being born."

Patricia France is a Bay Area native, born and raised. Inspired by her childhood and Oakland, she's written creatively on and off for several years. While enrolled in creative writing at Berkeley City College, she took a workshop with Sharon Coleman and decided to take poetry more seriously. Currently, she attends graduate school.

Shaun Freeland may or may not be a figment of the imagination . . . on most days he prefers to be, in any case. An avid consumer of literature, music, and guacamole, Shaun is currently traveling around the country and living out of a van, which he only sometimes parks by a river.

Amy Fukuizumi is a student of her surroundings. She studies Creative Writing at SFSU, love in her relationships and philosophy in her life. In writing, she finds her voice.

Laurin Gurrell was born and raised in the Bay Area. She completed her BA in performance studies and creative writing at Macquarie University in Sydney, Australia. Currently she resides in Oakland.

Scott Hoshida teaches at BCC and lives in Oakland with his wife and daughter. He studied creative writing at Mills and is working on a novel that has very little to do with rubber bands.

Tsutomu Inoue was born in 1975 in Kanazawa, Japan and left for Tokyo to go to Sophia University. After dropping out, he played guitar and wrote songs in a band called Highway 61, which released a major album with Warner Music, Japan. However, sales were bad, and the band broke up. He came to the U.S to study creative writing in 2010 and enjoys every moment at Berkeley City College. He's thirty-five and lives in Albany.

Natasha Ismail's philosophy is in alignment with her work as event coordinator and grant writer for Fertile Ground, a non-profit organization addressing the HIV/AIDS epidemic. "We must collect the memory of the ancestors for posterity."

Carla Kandinsky continues her student life at Berkeley City College, venturing into the study of modern art and other subjects not yet explored. Her recent poems appeared in Barbaric Yawp. She leads a memoir workshop at the North Berkeley Senior Center.

Kathryn Anne Kellogg managed to get a studio apartment before harming any of her roommates. When not plotting against people who eat the last of the Panda Puffs, she enjoys cooking (badly), reading (indiscriminately) and watching old movies (a little too much; it's a problem).

Jonathan Kwak is a graduate of San Diego State University and studied at L'academia Belle Arti in Firenze (The Academy of Florence) in Italy, from 1998-1999. Mr. Kwak was one of the recipients of Creative Capacity Fund from CCI, in 2010. His work has been shown in Italy, San Diego, and around the Bay Area.

Rosa Lane worked with Jane Cooper, Jean Valentine, Tom Lux, and Grace Paley at Sarah Lawrence. She is author of Roots and Reckonings and her work appears in Passages North, Dark Horse, Milvia Street, and Sarah Lawrence Review. With a PhD in architectural sustainability, she finds balancing writing with her commitment to sustainable architecture a constant challenge.

Willy Lizárraga was born and raised in Peru and arrived in San Francisco as a teenager. He has published short stories in the New South Journal of Art and Literature and ZYZZYVA. His novel in Spanish Mientras Elena en su lecho was published by the University of Miami. He teaches Spanish at BCC.

Linda Lu is a student of the Peralta Colleges. She produced this first published work through the creative writing class offered at Berkeley City College.

Michelle Lynné is an artist, poet, and writer with disabilities. She lives in Oakland.

Rachel Marcus is a native New Yorker living in Berkeley and embracing a lifestyle of yoga, fresh vegetables, and communing with nature.

Jess Marks-Gale studied Feminist Studies and Literature at UC Santa Cruz and become an excellent knitter and passable cook. After two years in AmeriCorps teaching literacy in Oakland, she's at the Mills MFA program. Milvia Street is her first publication.

Michael Noel spends summers in Paris and Cannes where he visits friends and slowly improves his shaky command of the French language. He works as a school psychologist and writes compulsively. Currently he's working on a comic mystery novella set in Paris.

Inna Nopuente is a creative writing student at Berkeley City College. She grew up in the Philippines where she visits once a year to idle on its beaches. Her poetry has appeared in Milvia Street.

Meredith Paige's work has appeared in The G.W. Review, Milvia Street and Elephant Journal. Her serial poem, The Ride Home, will appear in e-book in the next issue of Poecology. She lives in Oakland and teaches at Berkeley City College and the Art Institute of San Francisco

Isla Prieto is a self-taught artist with a BA in Liberal Studies from St. John's College. She designs media with original artwork for theater groups, musical events, and Pegasus Books. Her shows include Jigsaw Paws at Mamma Buzz in Oakland and Ora Universal at the Space Gallery in San Francisco.

Teneré Richmond lives in the Bay Are with his wife and child. He attends creative writing classes as Berkeley City College and plans to transfer to U.C. Berkeley to study linguistics.
Vinothini Sachithananthan was born and raised in Sri Lanka and migrated to the US four years ago. A collection of her Tamil poetry has been published in India. She writes poetry in Tamil and English and enjoys reading, drawing, and cooking.

This is **Mary K. Senchyna's** first publication. She works at San Francisco General Hospital as a psychiatric social worker and lives in Oakland where she is writing a memoir about her travels to Cuba to visit her husband.

Wattie Taylor: College! Become a physicist! Well? Fifteen years later, registered architect. Published for a cliff house on Fishers Island. Bored, carpenter thru 80's supporting his anti-nuke photojournalism in Europe. Next? California. Poetry? Why not?

Hao C. Tran (pronounced HOW) is writing passionately about post-war Vietnam with his real experiences and those from friends and family. He travels often and mixes business with flyfishing, photography, and creative writing.

Josephine Tsay is still in the exploratory stage with her artwork and is interested in the art of nostalgia: how to use traces of the past to inspire thoughts of the future.

Matthew Valencia is a 23 year-old BCC art student who uses various media, including charcoal, watercolor, gouache and acrylic. Matthew's specialties are landscapes, abstracts, transportation systems and food. He grew up in New York City and the San Francisco Bay Area.

Renate Valencia is a freelance food writer and business consultant by day. She studies painting at BCC and paints and draws by night.

Sharmini Wijeyesekera is currently fulfilling her dreams of being a traveling street musician/sometimes club performer. She likes to sprinkle her street performance with poetic wisdom learned from Tuesday night poetry class at BCC.